NARCISSUS IN TREATMENT

NARCISSUS IN TREATMENT
The journey from fate to psychological freedom

Richard I. Feinberg

KARNAC

First published in 2013 by
Karnac Books Ltd
118 Finchley Road
London NW3 5HT

British Library Cataloguing in Publication Data

A C.I.P. for this book is available from the British Library

ISBN-13: 978-1-78220-016-1

Typeset by V Publishing Solutions Pvt Ltd., Chennai, India

Printed in Great Britain

www.karnacbooks.com

To Bertie

CONTENTS

ACKNOWLEDGEMENTS

There are many people to acknowledge for contributing to the creation of this book. Among them are those that I have treated in psychotherapy, both past and present. I am deeply indebted to them for entrusting me with their innermost feelings and highly personal experiences. Working with my clients has deepened my experience and growth as a therapist as well as informed ideas contained in this book. In sharing the therapeutic process, I have learned from each one of them.

It is with great gratitude that I acknowledge colleagues who listened to my meanderings and offered invaluable comments on the text along the way. These include Lee David Brauer, Dianne Friedman, Bland Maloney and Jeanne Kleinman. I also owe a debt to mentors who educated and guided me. These include Bill Puka for his friendship and conversations about a philoso-personal approach to life, Drew A. Hyland for seminars on Plato and Heidegger, Miller Brown for his course on madness and civilization, the late Judith Mishne for explaining the nature of personality disorders, and Robert E. Simpson and Gerry Schamess for supervising me to grasp experience at its core for the sake of intervening effectively in treatment. I carry them with me in my professional life.

I want to thank all those at Karnac for their interest and efforts in bringing this book to publication. In particular, I am grateful to my editor, Rod Tweedy, for his encouragement and guidance.

The final acknowledgement is for the support of my family. I have deep appreciation for my daughters, Aleyna and Julie, and wife, Ellen, for providing caring, humor, insight, and patience to nurture my writing. It is a better book due to their involvement.

ABOUT THE AUTHOR

Richard I. Feinberg, Ph.D., is a psychotherapist in private practice in Bloomfield, Connecticut with over twenty-five years of experience. He received honors in Philosophy as an undergraduate at Trinity College in Hartford. He earned an M.S.W. from New York University and a Ph.D. from The Smith College School for Social Work. He has published articles on group therapy, psychoanalysis and existential analytic theory. His work has encompassed outpatient mental health clinics in Harlem and the South Bronx as well as private psychiatric hospitals—such as The Austen Riggs Center and The Institute of Living. He lives in northern Connecticut with his wife, two daughters, and three-year-old rescued Brittany spaniel.

PREFACE

As I note on the first page, this book has been some forty years in the making. It combines both personal and professional experience of what it is like to emerge from years of low self-regard, due to narcissistic injury, to ultimately achieve a sense of self-acceptance and psychological freedom. Rather than to delve into a personal memoir or reveal the emotional suffering of people whom I have treated in psychotherapy, I chose to focus on the dynamics of the narcissistic drama portrayed in D. H. Lawrence's *Sons and Lovers*. That astounding autobiographical novel contains all the elements of the narcissistic drama that a psychological work on narcissistic injury would need in order to demonstrate what it is and how it is perpetuated into adulthood. It readily and sensitively provides a picture for the reader as well as clinical material unobstructed by bias. The psychological torment of the main protagonist, Paul Morel, is something with which readers might empathize and identify.

In focusing on *Sons and Lovers*, it was an additional bonus to discover that the year, 2013, is the centenary of the first publishing of this novel. It is my hope that enthusiasts and students of D. H. Lawrence, as well as others, will find that observations in this book contribute to an understanding of this work at this important commemorative time.

The idea to write on this topic has been on my mind ever since my first reading of Alice Miller's *The Drama of the Gifted Child*. I shared the experience that many of my patients described after reading it. While it provides a beneficial theoretical framework about narcissistic injury, it does not explain how one psychically heals from it. It leaves the reader with pressing questions about how to deal effectively with emotional conflict and pain. To put it metaphorically, it is somewhat akin to undergoing surgery without being stitched up at the end.

A central aim of this book is to present the process of psychic healing from narcissistic injury through an understanding of therapeutic action. This presentation draws predominantly from the brilliant clinical and theoretical contributions of Hans Loewald and Jonathan Lear. I am indebted in particular to Lear's notion of irony and its role in facilitating structural change in the mind. It advances the conditions for psychic healing to occur. Lear addresses the concept of irony and its place in the therapeutic process in his remarkable book, *Therapeutic Action*. This incisive work has been a principal influence on me both professionally and personally.

Narcissistic injury is caused by the psychological domination of a child by a narcissistic adult. Invariably, the adult is the child's parent. Most children who are targets of narcissistic parents are often unaware, as they age, of the existence and scope of their emotional injury. It can be insidious. For those with some inkling about it, it is not wise or advisable to wage a rebellion against the narcissistic parent. A protracted battle may satisfy righteous indignation but only serves to further entrench the saga of domination within the mind. The only true psychological freedom can be achieved by the resumption of maturation through therapeutic action.

The final basis for this book is the desire to revive interest in the ground-breaking psychological work of Ludwig

Binswanger. His contributions to understanding human nature and efforts to minister human suffering have been buried by the relentless march of modern psychology and psychiatry in the name of science. It is my hope to renew attention to his work and generate appreciation for his humanitarian project.

CHAPTER ONE

Introduction

Framing the question

Forty years ago, I was startled by a story in the local news. It was about a high school senior from a small affluent town in metropolitan New York. He was a popular scholar-athlete, captain of the football team, headed for the Ivy League. It was late autumn. One Sunday afternoon, he went to the town green, sat down, doused himself in gasoline and struck a match.

The news of his immolation was shocking and, according to the report, took everyone who knew him by surprise. Why would someone so young, who had everything going for him, commit such an act? And to do it in such a violently spectacular way! Who wouldn't have been affected by the news of this event? It left me with a sense of horror.

There was an existential piece to my reaction. I had just been exposed to the writings of R. D. Laing, Rollo May, Albert Camus and Jean-Paul Sartre. As any newly intellectual, questioning, and episodically miserable high school senior would do, I pondered over ideas such as the meaning of death, suicide, and the futility of life. It is one thing to fantasize about self-immolation but quite another to actually go through with it. What tipped the balance to motivate him to commit

1

the act? Was it impulsive or planned? How wretched he must have felt beneath all of that conventional success. There were news items at the time about young Tibetan monks immolating themselves in protest against the Vietnam War and social injustice. Was his act one of protest? If it were, what would he be protesting? In the end, it is unthinkable. What led him to enact the unthinkable?

The article was brief and buried somewhere in the first section of the daily newspaper. It never made the local news on television. There was no report that a suicide note had been left. There was no explanation at all. He apparently didn't even tell his girlfriend. The funeral was private. As one would expect, the story received fleeting attention by those who even noticed. The tragic spectacle was quickly dropped and faded away. But it struck a deep emotional chord in me. I wanted to know what it was.

When news of the immolation hit me, my English class happened to be reading D. H. Lawrence's short story, *The Rocking-horse Winner*. The association of the immolation to this story was immediate and unmistakable.

The Rocking-horse Winner is about a highly narcissistic mother who engulfs her young son in her insatiability for money. She doesn't explicitly or directly demand it, rather, the boy experiences the entire home itself throbbing with his mother's need for money. He assumes, as his sole purpose, the aim of getting it for her. Through his contact with the gardener and his uncle, he learns about horseracing and the money that winning bets can bring. He conjures up a way of picking winning horses by frantically riding on his toy horse in his bedroom until he reached a vision of the names of future winners. With the assistance of the gardener and his uncle, he then placed bets to his mother's oblivion. Spectacularly and serendipitously, his efforts paid off—enriching him, the gardener, and the uncle. After accumulating a large sum of money, the boy had his uncle give it to his mother anonymously. He feared that she might reject it or be angry with him if she knew how the sum had been raised. His mother's pleasure at receiving the gift was transient. To the boy's surprise and chagrin, the home now throbbed even louder for more money. He realized that the more he won and the more money his mother received, the worse her insatiability would become. Still, he was committed to satisfying her needs and quieting the house. Beside himself with desperation when the vision of winners became more difficult to come by, his riding became more frenzied and ultimately sent him into a perilous fever. He lost consciousness and died. While his death takes the mother by surprise, she is constitutionally incapable of true grief. She lacked the capacity to appreciate the boy in the first place. The boy's death is yet another tragedy soon to be forgotten.

Death by fever is analogous to death by immolation. On one hand, the flames are internal and, on the other, external. In both cases, the flames are consuming. In the wake of reading *The Rocking-horse Winner*, the immolation took on added significance. What if the immolation was in fact a protest—a protest against being engulfed by a narcissistic mother in a world insatiable for achievement? What if he was never allowed to be himself in a real way, believing that there would be no prospect of ever achieving a sense of his unique self at some point in the future?

Years later, in my psychological reading, I came across a poignant passage in a paper by the British psychoanalyst, D. W. Winnicott. It made me recall the immolation. In describing what he refers to as a false self that utilizes a strong intellect to resolve deep emotional problems, Winnicott presents the following perplexing picture:

> The world may observe academic success of a high degree, and may find it hard to believe in the very real distress of the individual concerned, who feels "phoney" the more he or she is successful. When such individuals destroy

> themselves in one way or another, instead of fulfilling
> promise, this invariably produces a sense of shock in
> those who have developed high hopes of the individual.
> (Winnicott, 1960, pp. 140–152)

What did Winnicott mean by a "false self"? How could someone in the throes of this distress knowingly take measures to destroy themselves? What is this emotional distress about in the first place? And, is there a way out? These are a few of the questions that led me to conduct a search over time that encompassed personal experience, reading, seminars, and learning from others in my role as a psychotherapist. Could the immolation have been avoided if other reasonable options had been open or apparent to him? What might those options be? I set out on a personal and professional quest to explore these questions.

This book contains both the findings of this extended search as well as new realizations and questions that have arisen along the way. It is intended for a diverse audience. In an immediate sense, it is an effort to reach out to those who are at risk of, or are contemplating, or have already enacted meta-phoric self-immolation in one way or another that is not due to psychosis. In a more general sense, it is intended to appeal to the curiosity and psychological needs of adults who were children of narcissistic mothers in particular. It delves into their intermittent and often long lasting feelings of emptiness, poor self-esteem, loneliness, bleakness, and chronic self-critical awareness of not being "good enough". This self-criticism can encompass appearance, academic aspirations, financial goals, intimacy, and the quality of relationships to name a few. This gnawing sense of futility is, more often than not, mystifying to those who feel it. As witnessed in the case of the immola-tion, conventional success does not automatically confer a sense of wellness. Living with these self-critical feelings forces one to logically assume responsibility for harboring them in the first place. After all, the futility lies "in oneself" and so it is taken to be one's own and one's own alone. Though it can be a struggle to admit it to oneself, this corrosive self-criticism cannot be denied. Disappointment at not meeting expectations can be crushing.

Typically, as seen in *The Rocking-horse Winner*, children of narcissistic mothers devote their lives to compensating for perceived deficits. In so doing, they frequently hurl themselves tirelessly towards meeting or surpassing expectations that were never natively their own. Consequently, they set out on a course of life that is inevitably alienating—that is, alienating from their true emotional core. The fear of being or becoming a failure is harbored as a most closely held secret—only to be shared with those most trustworthy, if anyone can be trusted at all. Eventually, many of those enduring this constellation of thoughts and feelings find their way as adults at any stage to seek help out of this emotional morass through psychotherapy. Often, this is a path taken after much soul-searching, rumination, suffering, and other short-circuited attempts at striving to be effective with oneself. Though immediate symptomatic relief is desired and psychopharmacology offers its wares, the ultimate realization is that symptomatic relief alone or the fantasy of a quick fix is not the answer.

Adults who have been emotionally damaged by narcissistic mothers have experienced injury to the self in the process of its formation. This injury becomes compounded over time by continuing to live a life mediated through this very damaged self. Insecurity perpetuates insecurity. Although the road towards health can be daunting, it is vital not to lose hope. Lives emotionally damaged in this way can improve and prevail but only if the approach to healing and resolution takes into account the true nature of the psychic wounds. It is none other than the emotional sphere that requires attention. There needs to be an appreciation for and education about how a human being develops into a person. Conversely, there needs to be awareness and sensitivity to how this process can go awry.

One can view this search as more relevant today than it was forty years ago. The sense of urgency about it in contemporary society has escalated. Take the emotional and financial pressures confronted by high school seniors as an example. The obscene expense of a college education coupled with the vicissitudes of maturing into adulthood force them to prioritize expedience and practicality over growing up and becoming well-rounded and independently functioning young adults. The result has been the distortion of formative college years—that ultimately boil down to career development to justify or recoup the huge investment. The traditional overt mission statement of colleges and universities has, for the most part, become corrupted and usurped. Who could blame students for nervously fixing on career plans before entering college? The system necessitates it. One thing that has gone out the window in forty years is the notion that education can be for education's sake with an emphasis on new learning and self-discovery. For the vast majority of college freshmen today, the drive towards career planning eclipses a search of self-knowledge and growth. Courses and majors are selected as perceived prerequisites for entrance to the professions: pre-med, pre-law, pre-business, etc. The emotional risk in all of this tumult is that young people are compelled to take the one-dimensional route of career tracking rather than a multidimensional orientation towards college life. Fear and anticipation of the future eclipse needs in the present. There is the pervasive view that contemporary economic realities are so harsh that there can be no luxury to indulge in one's development as a multidimensional person. The economic realities are indeed harsh and that is unfortunate in terms of available options and opportunities for growth. A concern is that high school seniors and college freshmen are likely to make crucial and even binding life decisions without first developing their very lives themselves. The danger lies in the possibility of future dissatisfaction or even disillusionment about chosen career paths, jobs, locked-in expenses (such as student loans), marriage, and children. It is not difficult to envision how widespread self-alienation can ensue from this scenario.

Considering the plight of these young people reaffirms an awareness of how a developing sense of self is bombarded by standards, expectations, and parental aspirations. It is no wonder why many of them, in this context, are self-absorbed and self focused. They are not doing it exclusively or necessarily out of a sense of self-aggrandizement. They are either tending to emotional damage already incurred, warding off the prospect of potential damage in the future, or both. The uncertainty of the economy is constantly unsettling in itself. Parents are as much out to sea on these issues as their children. However, they invariably pay tuition or co-sign student loans. The pressure to make good on the financial investment as well as making one's parents proud can be immense. The pressure is multiplied many times over when the child is raised by a narcissistic mother.

It must be acknowledged that narcissistic fathers are certainly every bit as damaging as their maternal counterparts. Those who were children of a narcissistic parent virtually never reach adulthood emotionally unscathed. The primary focus in this book on narcissistic mothers is based arbitrarily on the specific case material chosen to demonstrate these dynamics. That case material is about to be introduced.

Literature is replete with images of narcissistic fathers. This theme is brilliantly and poignantly captured, for example, in the writings of Franz Kafka. His novella, *The Metamorphosis*, perfectly depicts the pervasive, persistent, and searing anguish of a son rejected with disgust by his father. In that work, the son is degraded to the form of a large, hideous, self reviling roach-like creature. Failing to achieve the standards and expectations of the narcissistic father leads the son to revile himself and develop a towering sense of guilt for merely existing. In Kafka's novel, *The Trial*, the protagonist knows that he has been pronounced guilty by the Higher Courts but, despite a vigorous search, never learns about the substance of the accusations against him. The stakes for the targeted child of a narcissistic father according to Kafka are as severe as those just seen in Lawrence's *The Rocking-horse Winner*. The torment of rejection of not being good enough can ultimately result in death.

The central psychological question pursued here is the following: How does a child of a narcissistic parent emerge to become an autonomous adult? The answer is explored throughout this book.

Rather than presenting a case from my psychotherapy practice, I have decided to turn to literature for clinical material to demonstrate what I refer to as narcissistic drama. The narcissistic drama is simply the emotional dynamic between a narcissistic mother and her narcissistically wounded child. The reasons for this approach are threefold. First, this choice protects the identities of my patients and honors their privacy. Second, it enables readers to have access to identical clinical information and history. As a result, it avoids the practical problem of having to view case material through my idiosyncratic lens. Therefore, one can draw one's own conclusions unimpeded by bias. Third, I gravitated to a literary masterpiece of incisive psychological intuition that exquisitely taps the depth and breadth of the narcissistic drama. That novel is D. H. Lawrence's *Sons and Lovers*. Published in 1913 when Lawrence was twenty-eight years old, it is an autobiographical work. The story centers on the emotional struggles of Paul Morel coming of age in a family dominated by a tyrannical mother.

* * *

The myth of Narcissus and Echo

The term "narcissistic" has been so frequently used in common language as to be vacuous in meaning. It has encompassed references from selfishness to boasting to mental disorders involving lack of connection to others. Psychiatric manuals are primarily descriptive on the subject and offer little as far as learning about the essential meaning of the term. In order to shed light on the meaning of "narcissistic", it is vital to turn to the popular ancient Greek myth itself. For the Greeks, myth and drama served a cathartic function regarding fate and punishment incurred by humans who dared to defy the gods in their excessive behavior. They provided cultural guidance cautioning against faulty judgment and instilled a sense of danger in veering from civilized conduct.

There are several renditions of the myth of Narcissus. The version cited here is from *The Metamorphoses* of the first century Roman poet, Ovid. The myth of Narcissus is a myth within a myth. It might more accurately be entitled the myth of Narcissus and Echo.

Narcissus is born to the river god, Cephisus, and the water nymph, Liriope. She asks the seer, Tiresias, if Narcissus will live a long life. Tiresias cryptically answers that Narcissus will die if he comes to know himself. With this, the prophesy of Narcissus' doom is predicted.

Narcissus becomes exquisitely handsome and, by the age of sixteen, is irresistible to all who behold him. Echo, the mountain nymph, becomes smitten by his beauty as he hunts in the woods. Echo has been doomed to repeat only the last three words spoken to her in the very voice of the speaker as a prior punishment levied by Hera. Hera instituted this punishment because Echo once obeyed Zeus' request to divert Hera's attention while he frolicked among the nymphs in the woods. Echo yearns to express her love for Narcissus but can only mimic him. Narcissus is repulsed by her and, believing that she would never be good enough for him, rejects her. Echo then wastes away in unrequited love while only her faint voice remains. When Echo's plight is repeated by yet another nymph, the latter nymph prays to the gods that Narcissus should be sentenced to endure the same consequences. Her prayers are heard and answered by Nemesis, the goddess of revenge.

Exhausted from hunting, Narcissus comes upon a pool of water shaded by trees. When he kneels to have a drink he beholds the reflection, initially unaware that it is his, and falls in love with it. Reaching in vain, he can neither hold it nor stop gazing at it. He goes without food or sleep and withers. When it is much too late, Narcissus realizes as prophesized what has become of him. Still, he cannot avert his gaze. He is dying from unrequited love. When Narcissus dies and the mountain nymphs search for his body, all that is left is a beautiful flower by the pool of water.

It is the themes of this myth that give dimension to the word "narcissistic". Narcissus is guilty of false pride or hubris, a grave sin according to the Greeks. It is false pride to conceive of oneself as godlike. Narcissus is guilty of false pride in considering himself superior to everyone in beauty, even the gods. As a grave character flaw for the Greeks, the sense of false pride is punishable by death. A second central theme is that of unrequited love. The Greeks knew that unrequited love manifests in obstacles to receiving love as well as to expressing love. Echo represents the former in the sense that her love was not returned by Narcissus. On the other hand, Narcissus was blocked in expressing love because the object of his love was elusive. The myth of Narcissus and Echo, therefore, is largely about being misguided in love and failing to connect with the loved object. Lastly, there is the element of revenge. Nemesis seeks vengeance against Narcissus both on account of false pride and unrequited love. Echo is the target of Hera's revenge for meddling with the gods. In the end, the term "narcissistic" is associated with severe deprivation. Narcissus literally perishes from the lack of food and water because he cannot free his gaze in order to live. Narcissus is punished for daring to be something that he is not.

This myth leads to an understanding of the term "narcissistic" as emotional deprivation arising from rigid preoccupation with one's self that precludes giving or receiving love. As such, it is an emotional wasting disease. One can gather that this deprivation is tragic not only for the narcissist but as well for those in the orbit of the narcissist's life.

* * *

The goal of autonomy

The last key term to be defined is autonomy. Developmentally, it is the first experience of emancipation from the mother. It is captured in the universal experience of a one year old overjoyed about taking his first steps on his own away from mother. It is a milestone marking the process of achieving separation and emergence from the mother-child dyad. This is fueled by the toddler's sense of healthy narcissism in being upright, mobile, and separated. Optimally, the support by his mother and others further consolidates the toddler's sense of omnipotence at this juncture.

The child of a narcissistic mother is by definition not allowed to be autonomous. The toddler's opportunity to separate becomes thwarted due to the mother's need to keep her child attached to her. Her self-centeredness undermines the child's developmental need to differentiate beyond the symbiotic relationship. Erikson explains that the child's failure at autonomy results in the experience of shame and doubt (Erikson, 1959, pp. 67–77). Observational studies of one-year-olds held by narcissistic mothers demonstrates an initial inclination towards protest and frustration in the rigidity of the child's body and in fits of crying (Mahler, Pine & Bergmann, 1975, pp. 95–105). Over time, these protests fade away due to the repetitive and mundane absence of attunement in the self-centered mother. Ultimately, compliance sets in as the child clearly learns to take its cues first from the mother. Rather than separating and differentiating, these children become narcissistic appendages of their mothers (Miller, 1981, pp. 34–39).

Winnicott's observation comes to mind in considering adult children of narcissistic mothers. If these children have the need to simulate autonomy as part of a false self, created to appease their mothers, then perhaps that explains why those with promise destroy themselves to the shock of others. Self-destruction can be seen as a protest against the narcissistic mother for crushing autonomy, the process of separation and the emergence of the true self in the child. This conclusion is borne out in *The Rocking-horse Winner* in the dynamic between the child and his mother.

In the case of freshmen in college, the experience of autonomy is essential to the emotional and intellectual exploration necessary for forming themselves and their lives. In an ideal world, autonomy would manifest for them as psychological freedom both towards exploration and away from constraint. As previously noted, the financial and career pressures pose disincentives to take a chance at exploration. In addition, these pressures constitute constraints on autonomy by making career choices the only priority. The desperation to succeed and make parents proud eclipses the value of autonomy and the prospect of taking the path towards real fulfillment. In the face of the current economic realities, there is at the same time a crisis of autonomy and the opportunity to meet developmental needs vital to generating a whole person. The risk of ignoring or deferring this process can lead to an experience of shame, doubt and self-alienation.

* * *

The narrator of Sons and Lovers

Sons and Lovers is a story told by a narrator who never identifies himself. The novel simply begins with the narrator's gloomy description of dreary landscapes and small homes of coal miners in a lower middle class town in England. He describes the miners as mindlessly and pointlessly burrowing in the ground like ants. It is the way, he informs us, to "Hell Row". The social commentary of this beginning provides an initial glimpse into the identity of the narrator as an astute observer. However, with the telling of the story, the presence of the narrator lies in the background and the reader instead finds himself readily engaged in the meanderings of the plot itself. This approach to storytelling is in contrast, for instance, with that of Melville in his masterpiece, *Moby-Dick*. In Melville's novel, the narrator boldly identifies himself in the very first sentence as Ishmael.

The importance of knowing something about the narrator in *Sons and Lovers* has to do with appreciating the perspective of the specific lens through which observations and reflections in the story are perceived. In other words, the story unfolds through the eyes of the narrator. Therefore, an awareness of the qualities of the narrator itself has impact on understanding the novel from both literary and psychological points of view. Ascertaining the structure of the narrator's lens has crucial significance in the effort to reveal the nature of experience itself in the novel. In framing the question about the way in which a narcissistically wounded child could emerge into an autonomous adult, it is essential to get close to pristine experience itself. In this phenomenological way, a deep understanding of the impact of narcissistic injury can be attained (Husserl, 1911, p. 93). One of the principal aims of this book is to expose the true nature of this narcissistic injury. Towards this end, knowing something about the identity of the narrator will provide more acute perception both of the narrator's experience and how the narrator experienced the experience of others.

From a strictly literary point of view, the narrator is an artistic creation of Lawrence's. It is a creative device through which the story is told. There is value in knowing about the narrator in order to further inform one's reading of the novel. However, from a psychological point of view, all perception is mediated through the lens of the narrator. In this sense, the narrator is a character in itself and a person. It is incumbent upon us to know something about who this person might be.

While there may be little benefit from a literary standpoint in associating the narrator with Lawrence himself, the psychological implications of this association are compelling. After all, the author wrote the novel in his twenties with the perspective of a young man in his twenties. Moreover, the protagonist of the novel, Paul Morel, is twenty-four years old as the novel ends. This parallel is not directed towards equating the narrator with Lawrence himself but to wondering whether the narrator reflects some function relevant to Lawrence himself. From the beginning of the novel, it is clear that the narrator is a keen observer of the environment and people. In fact, it is this quality of the narrator that is most apparent throughout.

Psychologically, the narrator comes across not as Lawrence himself but as an observing ego. Though this may not appear to offer a significant distinction, it provides an important glimpse into the narrator's lens itself. From a psychoanalytic perspective, the narrator as an observing ego tells the tale through the strengths and limitations of that very ego itself. The narrator merely describes experience and phenomena but does not possess a cognitive framework for understanding their meaning. His descriptions are pristine and independent of constraints by any school of thought. Although Freud's initial masterpiece, *The Interpretation of Dreams*, was published in 1900, there are no indications of psychoanalytic concepts in *Sons and Lovers*. However, the novel was written at a time of psychological breakthroughs in understanding the human mind.

The narrator is an observing ego of a young man in his twenties reviewing his agonizing experience of coming of age. *Sons and Lovers* can thus be taken as the literary attempt of this observing ego to document and call attention to the mental anguish endured over this time. In one sense, the novel reads almost as a first person account of this suffering. It is an exquisitely sensitive effort to record the torment of a young man whose mother would not permit him to become a separate individual in his own right. The significance of placing this observing ego as a young man in his twenties has great bearing on where the narrator lies in the life cycle. It stands to reason that the reminiscences of someone at twenty-eight would diverge markedly, for instance, from a person in his seventies. Viewing the narrator in this way illuminates the lens through which the story is told and the context for psychological observation.

CHAPTER TWO

The unconscious assassin

What it is

A severely narcissistic parent programmed to exploit a child for the gratification of his or her own personal needs and to see it through is referred to here as an unconscious assassin. It is the characterization of a self-absorbed parent at the extreme symptomatic end of the narcissistic spectrum. This parent holds the child selected for such treatment as a psychological captive, not permitting the child to separate as an individual on its own. The child is likely to grow up with the burden of knowing that autonomy amounts to defiance and uniqueness is anathema in the eyes of the narcissistic parent. Self-doubt and low self-confidence follow in time as part of this emotional profile. It is for the sake of this child on becoming an adult that the central question of the first chapter is raised—how a child of a narcissistic parent becomes autonomous.

D. H. Lawrence's *Sons and Lovers* was chosen as the clinical material for this book precisely because it contains a character that embodies the essence of the unconscious assassin. That character is Gertrude Morel, the protagonist's mother. The central character in the novel, Paul, is one of her sons whom she psychologically dominates. This domination is the story about how his coming of age was thwarted by forced loyalty towards her. The dynamics of their relationship throughout the novel typifies salient aspects of the narcissistic drama.

By definition, an assassin is consciously deliberate about who is to be assassinated. John Wilkes Booth assassinated Abraham Lincoln. Sirhan Sirhan assassinated Robert Kennedy. Assassinations are typically politically motivated turning points in history as evident from these examples. However, this is not always the case. The assassination attempt on Ronald Reagan's life by John Hinckley did not have a political basis. The story is that Hinckley operated under the delusion that he would impress the actress, Jodie Foster, by gunning down the President. This event still counts as an assassination attempt, despite the absence of political motives, because it targeted such a prominent political figure. Does this imply that the definition of an assassin is always connected to a political motive or figure?

The Oxford English Dictionary (OED) defines "assassin" as a person hired or instructed to maliciously destroy or murder, often a political or religious figure, by treacherous violence. The word "malicious" certainly suggests the intent to harm, and "intent" implies conscious awareness. What about the possibility of the presence of intent to harm that is not in conscious awareness?

It makes sense that the notion of an unconscious intent to harm needs to be explored. The OED defines the word "unconscious" specifically in terms of Freudian theory as "designating processes activated by desires, fears or memories which are unacceptable to the conscious mind and so repressed". The unconscious, therefore, is the key to understanding the paradox of intent to harm (through action) that is not within the bounds of conscious awareness. An unconscious assassin is, then, someone unaware of harboring an intent to harm, or murder, a designated person.

There is more involved in this working definition. Freud's discovery of the unconscious accounts for why destructive impulses are generally and normally kept from expression through action. Civilized society is predicated on each individual's capacity of mind to control awareness and expression of these impulses through development of intra-psychic defense mechanisms as well as conscious moral deliberation. Without the repression of these impulses, chaos and mayhem would pervade society. A distinguishing feature of an unconscious assassin, in contrast to others, is the tendency for destructive impulses to seep into action. Since it occurs outside of conscious awareness, there is no inclination to take responsibility for those actions or ownership of the impulses themselves. In this way, an unconscious assassin can be diabolical in inflicting psychic damage upon vulnerable and unwitting victims.

It stands to reason that, if unconscious assassins wreak so much havoc by their antics, they should be held accountable for their actions. While that sense of accountability is sought here, it is important to understand that this process is not simple. It is not as though unconscious assassins are criminals to be arrested for breaking laws. Their infractions are on a much more subtle psychological level. In addition, they often strike deeply and are concealed. Unmasking Mrs. Morel as an unconscious assassin in *Sons and Lovers* does not constitute a straightforward and obvious task.

The criteria for identifying the harm she inflicts on others are complex and, more often than not, beyond the capacity of her victims to grasp. It is astonishing that the only character who sees Mrs. Morel as psychologically destructive is Miriam. Miriam is Paul's main love interest throughout the novel. Their relationship proves to be awkwardly intermittent. It ultimately fails precisely because it challenged Paul's intense need to sustain a level of total devotion to his mother. Miriam knew all along that Mrs. Morel hated her for purportedly trying to possess her son. She realized that this was entirely a projection.

It was Mrs. Morel who thought in these terms out of her own need to dominate Paul. Paul confused Miriam's urge to protect him from his mother as possessiveness. It was Clara, later in the novel, who pointed out that he was wrong about Miriam in this regard. The pressure of Paul's symbiotic tie to his mother skewed his perception in this instance. Paul is frequently angry with Miriam for purportedly complicating his relationship with his mother. The vicissitudes of Paul and Miriam's relationship display Paul's internal obstacles towards intimacy due to his inability to separate emotionally from his mother. Miriam is aware of Mrs. Morel's diabolical nature in this respect. Yet, it turns out to be much more extensive than Miriam could ever have imagined. No other character, especially Paul himself, perceives Mrs. Morel as causing such enormous emotional carnage. Oddly enough, the narrator has Walter Morel, her alcoholic husband, carry on in dialect to expose his wife's cruelty. But his rants pass unnoticed and are dismissed as the ramblings of a deranged drunkard. In this way, the narrator offers a glimpse into the reality of Mrs. Morel's true nature and how it can be disregarded.

One wonders how it is possible for Mrs. Morel's true identity to have eluded all of the characters in the novel. In other words, how did she get away with it? Moreover, what are the implications for narcissistically wounded patients in our practices? How do their parents get away with it in the eyes of others? It raises concern about identifying unconscious assassins in everyday life.

Part of the charade lies in the fact that the unconscious assassin carries on without admitting to harboring destructive intent. Others are easily diverted by this charade as well. This means that the unconscious assassin operates insidiously in stealth, not apparent to others or himself. In a mundane way, the actual psychic carnage is ultimately explained away as mistaken and its cause consequently attributed to extraneous factors. Never is the outcome ascribed to the unconscious assassin himself. For example, Paul cannot understand why his relationship with Miriam fails and certainly does not associate it with his mother. According to Paul, the problem is that Miriam is not meant for him—or, in other words, that the problem is Miriam herself. It is as though the unconscious assassin were programmed to maim without the faintest awareness of the existence of the program itself. This realization is chilling. It suggests, as witnessed in *Sons and Lovers*, that unconscious assassins operate fully, openly and, more often than not, with impunity. It is what each narcissistically injured patient mentions in treatment—namely, that the world knows his narcissistic mother as engaging and delightful rather than as cruel and self-absorbed. This is why it is crucial for unconscious assassins to be unmasked. It is vital for victims and potential victims to be protected from exploitation or, perhaps, self-immolation. As one readily sees in *Sons and Lovers*, it is possible for everyone to overlook the gravity of the peril caused by the unconscious assassin. One aspect of the effort here is to assist those at risk in identifying the Mrs. Morels in their lives.

* * *

Hate

It is striking how often the word "hate" appears in *Sons and Lovers*. In fact, it pervades the entire novel. The narrator is not using it as a figure of speech. Hate means hate. It is important to un-demonize, demystify and normalize the word "hate". However polarizing, it is a legitimate and important core feeling affirmed by the narrator.

Mrs. Morel's character is marinated in hatred. The first object of hatred is her husband, Walter. She spurns him throughout the novel. She hates him for his commonness. She initially hates him for lying to her about the ownership of their house. She hates him most for trapping her in poor economic circumstances, well beneath what she considers to be her rightful station in life. Her rejection of him is constant and relentless. She brazenly imbued hatred for their father in being a laggard in each of her children. William and Paul, the main targets of her narcissistic ploys, grew up detesting their father. William in particular felt charged with the role of protecting his mother from his father's brutish attacks. There is no mention of Annie, the daughter, hating her father. Arthur, the youngest, also comes to despise his father whilst resembling him most in appearance.

Mrs. Morel is mired in self-righteousness and, so, remains oblivious to the way in which this campaign of hatred psychologically scarred the children. First, it deprived the children of a positive experience of a father, and it left Walter as an emasculated husk, driven hopelessly to drink. Second, it served to severely distort the children's emotional development on both pre-oedipal and oedipal levels. On an oedipal level, it confounded the resolution of the Oedipal complex by virtue of an unchecked sexual charge towards the mother. The result is to elevate the mother as vastly superior to the father. Formulated in another way, Mrs. Morel represents a phallic mother. In addition, superego formation is skewed, further disrupting development. William and Paul lack a sense of conscience about how bizarre it is for them to cleave to their mother as singularly and intensely as they do. Nonetheless, it is in the pre-oedipal sphere that the effects of this hatred are most far-reaching. In essence, the hatred is merely part of the systematic process by which Mrs. Morel dooms the children to perpetual absolute dependence on her. This is especially evident in the lives of William and Paul where hatred functions to keep them bound to her symbiotically. This obstruction and violation of developmental needs amounts to hatred directed towards the children. The way in which the unconscious assassin hates the narcissistically charged children is thus readily observed.

The narcissistic wounds suffered by William and Paul as children give rise to hatred towards their love interests as adults. Upon introducing Lily to his family, William is incapable of restraining himself from being caustic to her in the presence of his mother. In his mind, Lily counted as a threat to this symbiosis. Clearly, and in light of his early emotional training, he instinctively opted for his mother. The same dynamic is seen in the case of Paul. In his ruminations, Paul hated Miriam for making his mother suffer. This feeling was usually followed by a sense of guilt towards Miriam and an urge for reparation. There are indeed moments when Paul felt a rush of tender feelings towards her as well as a sense of humility. Nonetheless, Paul had to leave Miriam because his mother's narcissistic grip from within himself proved to be overpowering.

The quintessential instance of hatred comes towards the end of the novel cloaked in merciful intentions. Paul and Annie conspire to end their mother's suffering from terminal cancer by administering a lethal dose of pain medicine, morphine. Mrs. Morel was never directly consulted or informed about this decision. As a mercy killing, it stands nonetheless as murder. This denouement is payment in a sense for Mrs. Morel's own lifelong campaign of terror and hatred. Through this action, the hatred she fomented is revisited upon her.

D. W. Winnicott stands out among psychoanalysts for his attention to the reality and place of a mother's hatred for her infant. His ideas on this topic can be found in the short and clinically incisive paper, *Hate in the Countertransference* (Winnicott, 1947). Although this paper was originally intended to apply to the treatment of psychosis in children, it is relevant here as well. Winnicott stressed the profound challenge and difficulty treating children who were objects of their mother's hatred. He advised that these cases should be referred for treatment to experienced clinicians with access to good supervision. It is a testament to the gravity of this kind of emotional injury.

Winnicottt maintained the following: "I suggest that the mother hates the baby before the baby hates the mother, and before the baby can know that his mother hates him" (Winnicott, 1947, p. 200). This observation is certainly implied in *Sons and Lovers*. The children never have occasion to acknowledge their mother's hatred throughout the novel. Only through her mercy killing does their hatred remotely rear its head.

For Winnicott, it is not the mother's feelings of hatred towards the infant that are problematic but, rather, it is the tendency for them to be expressed. In other words, the feelings themselves are not pathological but actions based on those very feelings can be pathogenic. Winnicott emphasized that:

> A mother has to be able to tolerate hating her baby without doing anything about it. She cannot express it to him … The most remarkable thing about a mother is her ability to be hurt so much by her baby and to hate so much without paying the child out, and her ability to wait for rewards that may or may not come at a later date. (Winnicott, 1947, p. 202)

In considering instances in which the mother's hatred seeps out towards the infant, the action can come across as direct or indirect. Direct expression of hatred towards the infant constitutes emotional and/or physical abuse. The infant is helpless and undeserving of this crass treatment. Unconscious hatred, on the other hand, can be expressed indirectly. It can manifest in more subtle ways as lack of attunement to the infant. This subtlety, it should be known, is only from the perspective of an outside observer or the mother herself. It is not lost on the infant. Lack of attunement on behalf of the mother is experienced by the infant, driven by the need for relatedness, as an emotional deficit or failure of the dyad. It can take the form of maternal disinterest when the child is in an excitable state or as maternal intrusiveness as it is quiescent. In either case, the outcome of maternal failure results in what Winnicott refers to as psychic impingement on the child (Winnicott, 1947). It affects the child by interfering with its sense of aliveness, spontaneity, going on being. Repetitive maternal failure of this kind places intolerable stress on the infant's mind and interferes with the development of its structure. This observation provides a glimpse into Paul Morel's confusion, isolation, misperceptions, existential thrownness and even suicidal feelings. As an adult, he suffered terribly from the cumulative psychic impingements of his early childhood.

* * *

The narcissistic maternal deficit

Due to the infant's inherent thirst for relatedness, Winnicott maintained that an infant is not accurately seen in isolation but always as the infant and the mother (see D. W. Winnicott in Greenberg & Mitchell, Eds., 1983, pp. 191–194). On a recent visit to the Rodin Museum in Paris, one particular bronze sculpture caught my attention. It was entitled, simply, *Mother and Child*. The sculpture is the figure of a mother sitting and embracing her child. Their bare bodies are together in a reciprocal embrace. The child's face is fused to the side of its mother's face. The association in my mind to Winnicott's observation was immediate. Early in life, the infant has no face, so to speak, and it develops in time with differentiation. Initially, the infant is immersed in the primordial dyad with the mother. Its primitive mind is not distinct but fused to the mother's. This picture captures the absolute dependence of the child on the mother. Through growth, the child progressively achieves greater differentiation. In normal development, the mother-child symbiosis gives way to yield a child in its own right.

Winnicott refers to this total maternal preoccupation as good-enough mothering. It involves timely and reciprocal ordinary attentiveness that is adequate to meet the infant's needs. In so doing, it nurtures and supports the infant's spontaneous gestures and early sense of aliveness. Optimally, the infant invests its psychic energy in forming its mind through a process of going-on-being.

In order to promote differentiation in the infant, progressive maternal failure must occur. Good-enough mothering ensures that this "progressive failure" represents stress on the infant that is emotionally tolerable. Intolerable stress gives rise to psychic impingements. Repetitive impingements trigger the formation of premature intra-psychic defense mechanisms in the infant, diverting energy away from the process of structuring the mind.

Winnicott identified one consequence of repetitive impingements as the formation of a false self (Winnicott, 1960). In this case, the child is pressured to conform to the mother's agenda, wish, or gesture. The child's true self goes into hiding and is protected by a false self as a defensive construct. In addition to protecting the true self, the false self is dedicated to appease the mother at first and eventually meet the induced expectations of others down the road. There are varying degrees of falseness. In an extreme instance, the child misidentifies the false self as the true self. In this case, the actual true self is hidden from the child itself and the false self is then embraced by the mother as real. The implications for this child are clear and unfortunate. The true self becomes unseen by the narcissistic mother. The child faces a life mediated through falseness. It is a life ultimately devoid of aliveness. This dynamic is witnessed in *Sons and Lovers*. Mrs. Morel's persistence and determination to have her way left Paul (since childhood) stuck with an emotional center of gravity lodged in his mother. His emotional boundaries were indistinct, leading to his tendency to share his most private thoughts with his mother. He was oblivious throughout about this lack of boundary. As a young adult, his intimate relationships were complicated by self-alienation and defensive over-intellectualization. With the death of his mother, Paul was utterly lost. By that point, the false self had lost its sense of purpose and the true self was adrift. For better or worse, he was finally on his own.

Through observational studies with mothers and their infants and toddlers, Mahler characterized the major milestones of early intra-psychic development as the process of separation–individuation (Mahler, Pine & Bergmann, 1975, p. 39). According to this theory, this process encompasses the sub-phases of differentiation, practicing, rapprochement and the inception of object constancy. Development can be derailed at any or all sub-phases given maternal deficits or stressful circumstances. In order to explain the origin of personality disorders seen in adults, Mahler and her team paid particular attention to disruptions at the sub-phases of practicing and rapprochement.

With the onset of walking, the one year old toddler is exhilarated and at the peak of its powers. A limitless and fascinating new world opens up for discovery and exploration. The toddler's first steps are away from his mother. In physically separating from his mother, the toddler is in the process of emotionally separating from his mother as well. It captures the toddler's emergence from symbiosis. Mahler noted that during the latter part of the sub-phase of practicing, when the task of walking had been mastered, the toddler tends to pause in its adventures to look back at his mother.

This tendency leads to the next sub-phase, rapprochement, in which the toddler experiences fear in being uncomfortably at a distance from her mother in its wanderings. This fear represents the toddler's need for what Mahler calls emotional refueling. How the mother treats her child during rapprochement has important implications for the toddler's capacity to develop autonomy. Good-enough mothering at this stage involves acknowledgement and support of the toddler's need in this respect without concern that the toddler might be regressing or that dependence is being encouraged. Mothers who are not attuned to their toddler's needs in this way may lack empathy and become annoyed with what appears to be an indication of regression. The lack of empathy and support at rapprochement constitutes developmental failure that thwarts the toddler's process to become emotionally separate from her mother. This is the basis for Paul's attachment in adulthood to his mother. As Erikson maintains in his stage theory of the life-cycle, deficits in autonomy give way to pronounced feelings of shame and self-doubt. This is not the formula for emancipation from the mother.

It has been shown that the narcissistic mother overpowers the child, forcing it to meet her personal needs. Her control is absolute and non-negotiable. The targeted child is the one receiving the greatest emotional investment from his mother. This child is invariably treated either as a narcissistic appendage of the mother or controlled through an "umbilical" connection. Our patients describe their narcissistic mothers' involvement in the following way: "It's all about her" or "It's her way or the highway" or, analogizing their mother to city hall, "You can't beat City Hall". Children prevented from psychologically separating live at their mother's beck and call (the appendage mode), or feel the pull of a taut umbilical connection. In both cases, the normal process of separation–individuation is blocked. By targeting a child for this treatment, the narcissistic mother severely interferes with the child's capacity to continue forming his own mind. The narcissistic mother is steeped so deeply in self-gratification that violating her child's integrity, individuality, and right to personhood is not even a passing consideration. The child is forced to conform because the narcissistic mother will have it no other way. The motivation behind this exploitation is none other than hatred on an unconscious level. This is what defines the narcissistic mother as an unconscious assassin.

Mrs. Morel married at age twenty-three and gave birth to her first child, William, at age twenty-four. In all, she had four children—a son, a daughter, and then two more sons. The novel begins dramatically with the birth of Paul, the third child. At the time of his birth, Mrs. Morel is thirty-one years old and already ministering to William and Annie. Paul was born both small and frail, unlike his older brother and father. Mothering did not come naturally to Mrs. Morel. It made her weary. Her main preoccupation was to lament over her dreary life, lack of money, and lowly station. When Paul was eight months old, she conceived her fourth and last child, Arthur. In her mind, Arthur's birth was purely for economic reasons. Arthur was born as Paul's need for attachment was at its peak. It is a foregone conclusion that his needs in this respect could not adequately have been met. As a consequence, Paul's unmet need for attachment persisted in his personality and provided his mother with emotional leverage to control him. Mrs. Morel trained her sons to bolster her lot in life by providing her with money. Both William and Paul went to work by the age of thirteen and dutifully turned over their earnings to her. Mrs. Morel hated her husband for squandering his meager income at the pub. Her craving for money parallels the mother's in *The Rocking-horse Winner*.

The terms "targeted" and "narcissistically charged" have been used to identify the specific child chosen for exploitation by the narcissistic parent. It is evident in *Sons and Lovers* that Mrs. Morel did not treat her children equally. The targeted children enveloped by the narcissistic drama were William and Paul. While Annie and Arthur did not receive the same treatment, they certainly did not get by unscathed. Their fate was abandonment. Essentially, they were irrelevant to Mrs. Morel's quest for financial security.

The first major challenge to Mrs. Morel's formula for security came when William announced his intention to leave home and seek his success in London. At first, William found work in London and loyally sent a portion of his wages to his mother. These installments gradually diminished as his life in London with Lily took shape. William had his own expenses, much to his mother's chagrin. Mrs. Morel directed her fury about the shortfall towards Lily. As time passed, William unknowingly underestimated the peril of overstretching the umbilical connection to his mother. In a psychological developmental sense, William ventured to separate from his mother before he was psychically prepared to do so. Ultimately, his life in London severed this umbilical connection and put his very life at risk. He had been much more psychologically dependent on his mother than he had ever known. With breathtaking suddenness, William fell ill, febrile and precipitously died. Embedded in William's death is the narrator's sense of caution about the dire stakes for the targeted child in defying the narcissistic mother. These are the same stakes seen in *The Rocking-horse Winner*. The gravity of the narcissistic drama is captured in tragedy and death. It is a kind of self-immolation.

Mrs. Morel's reaction to William's death further confirms her true colors. While it was William who succumbed, Mrs. Morel cast herself as the victim. She perpetuated the persona of the grieving mother, ostensibly pining over the loss of her eldest son. In actuality, her grief was not so much for William as it was for the loss of the income stream that he provided for her. She instinctively and immediately turned to Paul with a vengeance to make up for what was lost to her in William. Paul proves to be no match for her and is easily and willingly dominated by her. Although this evolution is not apparent to Paul, it is to Miriam. The domination of Paul by his mother is so daunting and complete that he has no choice but to extrude Miriam from his life. Mrs. Morel, as an unconscious assassin, is responsible for this tragedy.

* * *

Oedipal vs. *pre-oedipal*

It has been mentioned that the most far-reaching emotional damage to Paul occurred at the pre-oedipal level. This claim requires a bit more explanation. To be sure, oedipal issues also inhere in *Sons and Lovers* but are not as determinative of character.

In general, conflict at the oedipal level entails issues of competition, challenge, striving for success, and the suppression of sexual feelings/fantasies towards the parent of the opposite sex. The oedipal level always involves others (that is, mother, father, etc.) as discrete people in the child's world. Oedipal issues occur on a verbal level. In terms of the lifecycle, the resolution of the oedipal conflict takes place around the age of five. In contrast, pre-oedipal issues are generally ascribed to the first two years of life. They consist of matters of attachment, separation, dependence, integration, and regulation to name a few. Pre-oedipal experience occurs exclusively in a preverbal sphere. The context solely involves two people—the infant or toddler and the mother.

The central Oedipal fear is of castration or failure in some way. Mrs. Morel's systematic and relentless criticism of her husband, Walter, sealed his fate as an emasculated failure. She was too powerful and effective in this respect, leaving him without recourse. The primary fear on the pre-oedipal level is of un-integration and annihilation due to abandonment or object loss. This is Paul's predicament, certainly, when his mother fell morbidly ill and died. He became confused, overwhelmed, crushed, and completely lost. Unresolved castration anxiety can lead to despair. Unresolved anxiety at the pre-oedipal level can lead to psychic breakdown and even death. William's fate is indicative of this outcome.

Oedipal themes abound in *Sons and Lovers,* as seen in the campaign of sustained hatred towards Walter Morel. It is no surprise as well that Paul gravitates towards Clara, an older and estranged married woman. Clara's estranged husband, Baxter Dawes, is presented as a common drunkard who was never a good match for her. The parallels to Paul's parents are obvious. At the height of their involvement, Paul is twenty-three and Clara, thirty. Mrs. Morel never felt threatened by Clara for an array of reasons—not the least of which was Paul's lackluster attraction and attachment to her. In a blatantly oedipal challenge, Dawes pummeled Paul. In losing badly and suffering bruises, Paul experienced a counterbalancing outcome to the conflict that occurred in his family. Ultimately, Paul befriended Dawes as his interest in Clara dwindled. One might take this as a sign of Paul's wish on some level to reconcile with his father and set the oedipal conflict straight.

* * *

Guilt and responsibility

Is it legitimate to hold Mrs. Morel responsible for the havoc she caused if she was unaware of her intent and incapable of grasping the consequences of her actions? And what about consideration for Mrs. Morel as a victim of her own parents' transgressions? It would seem fair to take into account the likelihood of her turbulent background. Otherwise, the lack of balance runs the risk of simply giving Mrs. Morel a bad rap. While she did damage her children, she does not come across as either sadistic or an evil genius.

It would not be unexpected to learn that Mrs. Morel's narcissistic personality stemmed from emotional deprivation suffered during her own less than optimal beginnings. As suggested earlier by Winnicott, Mrs. Morel learned to hate from having been hated. It can reasonably be assumed that Mrs. Morel's own emotional straits point to intergenerational transmission of disturbed personality patterns. However, the narrator does not take time or interest to delve into it. As a result, it renders Mrs. Morel's character unsympathetic. In addition, Mrs. Morel's narcissistic tendency towards hatred can be seen as a displacement for hating prior frustrating objects. When her children do not gratify her narcissistic needs, her hatred of her depriving mother or father from childhood becomes visited upon them. While Mrs. Morel's plight is of concern from a systemic point of view, it has little bearing on the task taken up here. In terms of *Sons and Lovers*, the task is to lay out the nature of Paul's emotional predicament—what it is, how it came to be, how it was handled and what the possibilities may be for resolution. Mrs. Morel is not being held responsible for her actions in a legal sense. Rather, her accountability is sought from psychological and moral standpoints.

An initial consideration pertains to determining whether or not Mrs. Morel is psychotic. Is she competent to distinguish right from wrong? Clearly, it would not be possible to hold her accountable if she were psychotic. An example of this state of mind would be the presence of thought disorder, delusions or hallucinations instructing her to torment or kill her children. In *Fear and Trembling*, Kierkegaard alluded to these very circumstances with regard to Abraham. One recalls from the Old Testament that God instructs Abraham to sacrifice his son, Isaac, on Mount Moriah. Isaac is the embodiment of the covenant between God and Abraham. From a strictly ethical point of view, Abraham's intention to sacrifice Isaac amounts to murder. In twenty-first century America, any father prepared to kill his son on instructions from God would be considered insane. Contrasting Abraham's frame of mind with Mrs. Morel's unconscious intent is of course preposterous. However, it serves in the extreme to demonstrate a point. Abraham acted on fervent religious belief. Mrs. Morel acted on impulse and instinctive fear, justified by idiosyncratic conviction. Kierkegaard referred to the transcendence of ethics in the case of Abraham as the teleological suspension of the ethical. Mrs. Morel's case does not transcend ethics.

The contrast between Abraham's test of faith and Mrs. Morel's campaign of terror additionally centers on the capacity for reflection on the nature of a self that can reflect on itself. According to Kierkegaard, Abraham fully understood what God was asking of him. It is for this reason that each step he took towards Mount Moriah was filled with fear and trembling. Abraham's experience was embedded in constant reflection. The intensity of this reflection reached a peak as he raised his knife above Isaac's throat. In Kierkegaard's eyes, the sacrifice of the ram rather than Isaac enabled Abraham to experience Isaac returning to him anew—that is, Abraham experienced a new affirmation of the covenant with God. His reaction therefore was not simply one of relief. This is why Abraham is considered a towering religious figure or a Knight of Faith in Kierkegaard's terms (Kierkegaard, 1843, pp. 126–132).

In many ways, it is not surprising that Mrs. Morel's experience is antithetical to Abraham's. The most accurate depiction of Mrs. Morel's moments of self-review is of being haunted. As he languished in infancy, Paul haunted his mother through the pain in his eyes. It exposed her lack of empathy or interest in mothering at all. Throughout *Sons and Lovers*, she often pays homage to being haunted by her own unrestrained intrusiveness into the romantic lives of William and Paul. In this sense, she is aware of her narcissistic drive to turn her sons against their lovers. Finally, she is haunted by concealed guilt over William's demise.

One wonders whether being haunted counts as reflective activity on Mrs. Morel's part. My view is that these ephemeral moments of conscious awareness pass by in a flash, go absolutely unheeded and are ultimately discarded. It is the narrator who draws our attention to them. Mrs. Morel acknowledges them in her own ruminations. In the end, these moments are not taken as opportunities for worthy self-reflection. Time after time, she casts off any lingering awareness of her own feelings and disregards the consequences of her actions. It is due to her penchant for denial that Mrs. Morel is responsible in a psychological sense for the havoc she wreaks. She is deliberate in lacking curiosity about her self-absorption, her hatred of others, her ravenous envy towards her sons' romantic interests, and undermining the lives of William and Paul. Her actions are volitional and there is no evidence of psychosis.

Mrs. Morel consistently turned away from the misery she generated. She was never able to bear the reality of the carnage open-eyed. If she were to face her culpability, it would surely place her in the pantheon of the most guilt-ridden figures in Greek tragedy. *Sons and Lovers* is dominated by tragedy. In Mrs. Morel there is an eerie absence of anything maternal. There is no urge for reparation because there is nothing in her eyes requiring repair. There is no empathy for the child. The child's own most aliveness never gets supported, no less celebrated, by her.

* * *

Selection of the term "unconscious assassin"

In characterizing the pre-oedipal damage inflicted by Mrs. Morel on her children, Ruderman chooses the term "devouring mother" to denote how she engulfed her children to satisfy her own narcissistic needs (Ruderman, 1984). This description captures the image of an oral aggressive mother swallowing her child. The targeted child's predicament is further deepened by its helplessness in bearing a wish to merge with his mother in a symbiotic unity. As seen earlier through Winnicott, the threat to the child inheres in the pressure to conform to the mother's wishes leading ultimately to annihilation of the true self.

Ruderman's characterization of the devouring mother illuminates the intensity of the narcissistic drama and the significance of the stakes in a most visceral way. It is absolutely true that Mrs. Morel devours her sons at the pre-oedipal level and metabolizes them emotionally to become a part of her. In so doing, she virtually guarantees the impossibility of successful separation–individuation. The term "devouring mother", however, appears to me to have derived from a perch of objectivity on the narcissistic drama; that is, it involves perceiving the dynamic from outside of the targeted child's experience. While Ruderman's perspective is accurate and legitimate, it leaves aside a characterization of this dynamic from the child's point of view so to speak. The term "unconscious assassin" strives to encompass the image of the narcissistic mother in the eyes of the targeted child. It captures the directedness of unconscious destructive urges in the mother aimed specifically at the child. As repressed, these urges are not overtly evident to others or even to the mother herself. While the quality of the mothering may be considered attentive from without, the child knows the difference. The child emotionally reacts to the mother's unconscious. The child grasps very early that he is a target of his mother as an assassin.

The word "assassin" identifies the specificity in targeting a child for exploitation. From the infant's point of view, this hatred does not occur at random. It is defined by the quality of directedness. The infant apprehends that the hatred is aimed directly at him. The passage of time only seems to confirm this sense of specificity as unmistakable. It is at the root of the child's question in this drama: Why me? An assassin aims for a specific target and that is the basis for choosing it as a term. William and Paul are the targets of Mrs. Morel's insatiable narcissistic drive in the novel. It is from their point of view that she is seen as an unconscious assassin. As noted earlier, the children who were not targeted in this way are ultimately abandoned out of apathy. It does not end well for any of these children.

CHAPTER THREE

Paul's predicament

Thwarted separation

As I set out to write this chapter, I came across the obituary of Adrienne Rich in *The New York Times* (28 March 2012). She died at the age of eighty-two as a major figure in modern poetry. What was particularly striking to me in the obituary was her vision of a more perfect world—namely, one in which there is no domination of others. This idea is embedded both in her poetry and political convictions. A similar sentiment has been attributed to Bertolt Brecht who mused in a different way that the history of the world is about those who will be eaten and those who will eat. Domination fosters oppression. Oppression fosters alienation and enslavement, and enslavement is the greatest disgrace that can be foisted on human beings. Rich was addressing both psychological and political spheres. It is the psychological implication of domination that is taken up here.

The narcissistic drama is ultimately a story about domination. The newborn is in a state of absolute dependence on the narcissistic mother. What does this mean in terms of domination? Obviously, the power differential between the infant and her adult mother is so unimaginably colossal as to be incomprehensible. The infant is completely emotionally pliable. He has absolute dependence on the mother and the mother holds his aliveness in her hands. Good-enough mothering, according to Winnicott, implies that abuse of this power by the mother is unthinkable. It does not require special capabilities or giftedness. For Winnicott, good-enough mothering is extraordinary for being fundamentally ordinary. Primary maternal preoccupation is also borne out in observational studies done by Mahler. Good-enough mothers demonstrate basic maternal intuition towards their infants as "other"—that is, beings other than themselves that are absolutely dependent upon them. Ordinary mothering is not only the birthright of the infant. It is the most valuable gift that one human being can give to another—namely, the emotional acknowledgement of being truly alive as a being unto itself.

It has already been shown that the infant makes use of good-enough mothering by pouring her primal psychic energy into the gradual process of structuring its mind. Optimally, the mother-infant dyad evolves inexorably through "hatching" into greater differentiation. The process of emotional separation from mother constitutes psychological achievement leading to the child's eventual recognition of herself as a person. Human growth and development are inextricably bound to occur in the context of relationship—namely, the mother-infant dyad. The quality of the child's start in life is completely dependent upon the nature and quality of this dyad.

Psychoanalytic developmental theory holds that the infant introjects the mother and the dyad itself as mental representations in his mind for purpose of regulating drives, stresses, and structuring the mind itself. What does this mean experientially? It means that, in order to constitute itself, the primitive mind orients itself to "inner" and "outer" phenomena (though this distinction is not evident to the infant) for the sake of basic regulation and survival. At the beginning, the infant "takes in" the image of the breast as a means of regulating tension around hunger and subsequent frustration. The mental representation of the breast becomes an image in the infant's mind, apart from the actual breast itself. Consequently, the development of the infant's mind is set in motion both by the breast of "outer" reality and by its mental representation as an "inner" reality. These dual spheres, so to speak, arise from the psychophysiology of survival—the need to feed or perish, the need to engage immediately in relationship (with mother) or perish. In point of fact, there is no inkling of perishing in the beginning—only a drive to live. The thrust to relate at birth or instantly engage in relationship is viewed by Fairbairn as an aspect of psychological/ biological innateness (see W. R. D. Fairbairn in Greenberg & Mitchell (Eds.), 1983, pp. 151–187).

The development of the primitive mind brings us back to initial considerations about domination. In normal development, the child incorporates an image of the good-enough mother into his mind. This image actively participates within the infant's mind to contribute to the forming of that very mind. In other words, it promotes growth and development.

The question then arises as to what takes place in development when the mother is narcissistic and constitutionally incapable in a sense of engaging in primary maternal preoccupation? What happens to the infant? What are the ramifications in terms of the formation of the infant's mind?

The narcissistic mother's ideas and attitudes are taken up by the infant's mind as a toxic introject. This emotional toxicity does not kill the infant but perpetually oppresses it. The challenge confronting the infant in his early life is not only to face the actual un-attuned mother of "outer" reality but additionally to manage the image of the un-attuned mother taken into its mind. Psychic energy that would otherwise be directed towards developmental needs is siphoned towards frustration/aggression and the formation of primitive unconscious defense mechanisms. For children who do not succumb to severe outcomes such as psychosis, psychological damage manifests in a variety of ways.

In addition to the actual reality-based impingements endured during the first two years of life, the child is subjected to ongoing stress and pressure from the toxic introject in its "inner" emotional world. The crucial point is that the toxic introject, as a mental representation, remains immutably and tirelessly active in the child's mind as he develops through adolescence into adulthood. The child, adolescent, and adult, experience the presence of this toxic introject through guilt and self-criticism. This is the origin of the feelings of worthlessness so often heard from narcissistically injured adults in psychotherapy. It is important to note that adults wounded in this way initially perceive the basis for this suffering as self-referential; that is, one ascribes "badness" to oneself rather than displaying an awareness of the workings of the toxic introject. What is insidious about the activity of the toxic introject, operative at any moment as unseen or repressed, is the way it leaves the adult with battered self-esteem and depression. The toxic introject can be oppressive to the point of condemnation so that suicide arises as a possible consideration.

The toxic introject manifests in adults as an archaic entity—that is, it persists as the primitive introjected mental representation of the narcissistic mother from the person's infancy. Therefore, the archaic toxic introject is carried into adulthood unaltered by time. The distortions of self-criticism and self-recrimination reported by afflicted adult patients reflect the extreme behavior and unconscious content of the mother's mind passively absorbed by them in infancy. The source of confusion often experienced by depressed adults is in part a sense of confusion about the experience of time itself. Though they experience depressive symptoms in the present, the cause of this suffering is buried in the past. Therefore, it is at first unidentified. Through effective psychotherapy, it becomes apparent that feelings of rejection arise in their own minds as a result of the archaic toxic introject. Certain questions then come to the fore: how does one overcome, outgrow, or somehow detoxify the toxic introject? Or, at the very least, how does one master it in one's own mind in order to attain some semblance of freedom? Therapeutic approaches offering psychic relief by altering the content of thought do not provide lasting resolution. True psychic healing entails confronting the archaic toxic introject directly. That is achieved through effective psychoanalytic psychotherapy.

Domination by narcissistic mothers does not require militarism or physical oppression. Rather, it is accomplished by controlling the child from within her own mind. This leverage is exploited by inducing feelings of guilt in the child for wanting something for herself. In *Sons and Lovers*, Mrs. Morel manipulates William and Paul by reactivating the archaic maternal introject in their minds. The sons are controlled from within their own minds. It is for this reason that the issue of psychological separation inheres in their demise. As young men, neither William nor Paul demonstrates evidence of attaining emotional separation from their mother in their minds. They were oblivious to this reality and, additionally, never consciously ascribed malevolent domination to her. This enabled her to dominate in a stealthy manner. As already noted, it is a hallmark of the unconscious assassin.

Self-absorbed mothers are not, by definition, predisposed to seeking a common wavelength of emotional communication with their infants. Rather, they impose their wavelength restrictions onto the infants. This aspect of domination is not lost at all on the infant. It has been shown that the infant is pressured to conform to the mother's preference. Endless repetitions of this pattern lead to a reactive posture of compliance in the child. Over time, her protests are not heard by the mother and slowly fade. This experience is pulled out to sea by the waves of time. Adults struggling with the vestiges of this dynamic lament in treatment over being excessively accommodating in relationships or at work.

There are three categories in which adults that were narcissistically injured as children fall:

First, *the realization of the parental ideal*. In this case, the adult is subsumed by a total identification with the narcissistic mother. The archaic toxic maternal introject is so overpowering and engulfing that the primitive ego is too weak in comparison to resist being taken up into it. Repression and the repression of the repressed are complete to the point of wiping out any trace of observing ego regarding this dynamic in adulthood. These adults are automatons totally directed by their toxic introjects. They are often refractory to treatment in psychotherapy since there is no autonomous ego with which a therapist can ally. Another obstacle is seen in the fact that conventional success and achievement only serve to reinforce this self-alienating way of life. These individuals are inextricably tied to their mothers and the notion of autonomy is anathema. The fact that relationships outside of the toxic dyad may suffer is typically minimized as unimportant or not consequential. These people keep their stride in the face of perceived losses, which are never experienced as true losses. The notion that this is a wasted empty way of life never occurs to them.

Second, *an awareness of compliance joined to a sense of compromise and resignation*. These narcissistically injured adults do retain enough of a modicum of observing ego to sustain an awareness of psychological defeat on a conscious level. They recognize that they are dominated from without and within. The source of power is distributed equally between the actual mother and the toxic introject. These people live by the creed "You can't beat City Hall". Any inclination towards protest or struggle has long been muted in their lives. Their sense of resignation is founded on the certainty that the narcissistic mother is unassailable. Consequently, they make the enormous sacrifice of abandoning any hope for autonomy and respect as discrete individuals. These narcissistically wounded adults present in psychotherapy with deflated self-confidence and crushed self-esteem. The remnants of their observing egos are capable of capturing their lives as unlived and wasted. Their fundamental conclusion is that emotional separation from the narcissistic mother is futile and nothing will ever change.

Third, *an awareness of alienation from oneself, emotional injury, self-doubt, and self castigation.* As one can detect, this narcissistically wounded adult has retained enough observing ego to know that something went radically wrong in development. The initial awareness is not of the narcissistic drama but of feeling defective. Agonizing questions abound, such as "What is wrong with me?", "Why do I feel so miserable and self-rejecting?", "Why do I feel so alone, so empty?", "Doesn't anyone hear my cries for help?", "Why can't I take pleasure in any achievement?" and, "Why do I feel that I am never good enough?". One arrives at the conclusion that abject misery is due to being "bad" for any array of reasons. Since the narcissistic drama is not on a conscious level at first, self-blame prevails. This impasse results from the sheer intensity of the psychic pain and the fact that knowledge about the narcissistic injury itself still needs to be reached. Insight and intellect contribute to a search for understanding. Those fortunate enough to find their way enter psychotherapy or gravitate to books that shed light on these dynamics. The conclusion reached by these adolescents and adults is that their lives represent fractured efforts at emotional separation and autonomy. Their lives are not lost as much as they are tragic.

It is, however, this last category that contains individuals most capable of character change. The capacity to experience enlightened misery in this way presumes the existence of sufficient ego strength to contain the intensity of these emotions and initiate a willingness to conduct a search. There is an inclination to put mental suffering into words and seek the understanding and support of a therapist. The restitution of one's self-esteem is then a function of the new dyad that consists of the patient and the therapist.

It should not come as a surprise to learn that the vast majority of people who eventually become psychotherapists emerge from this category. Much of the incentive to become a psychotherapist arises from the psychotherapist's personal journey in overcoming early emotional conflict to become more autonomous adults themselves. This therapeutic experience serves to deepen and enhance their capacity to empathize with others. A great deal of knowledge and experience are acquired along the way that gives rise to interest in the development of the mind and an urge to facilitate emotional growth in others. The practice of psychoanalytic psychotherapy then becomes in part an ever-evolving affirmation of the psychotherapist's quest for emotional growth in oneself and others. This practice is nothing other than psychological midwifery.

In terms of *Sons and Lovers*, the narcissistic drama that inheres in William and Paul as young adults falls into different categories. William's suffering is representative of the first category. His ego has been totally subsumed by the archaic toxic maternal introject. As the first-born male at his young mother's mercy, William helplessly fell prey to her domination. From his youth, William was a narcissistic appendage of his mother. He never experienced an authentic sense of autonomy. Therefore, as an adult, his ego was too weak in daring to defy his mother by moving to London. Despite complying in sending her money, his attempt at separating from her was more than he could bear in the end. While he left for London as a strong, strapping young lad, he withered and died precipitously. It was as though he lacked a psychic immune system. William never actually stood on his own as an individual. His lack of awareness led to his death.

Paul faced a different predicament. Although he was frail and nearly died from an advanced pneumonia, he did not succumb to death. Paul's suffering, which constitutes the novel in its entirety, is characterized by the third category. *Sons and Lovers* is replete with acutely sensitive depictions of Paul's anguish. While he is aware of his misery, he remains oblivious throughout to his mother's manipulations. Like his older brother, Paul hates his father. However, evidence of pliability in this hatred is witnessed both in his challenge to and ultimate reconciliation with Baxter Dawes. It is important to note that Paul retains enough ego strength to neutralize the toxic effect of the maternal introject and evaluate others in the world. His meanderings with Clara and Dawes reveal a reworking of early conflict with his parents. His resilience in this regard is astonishing given the frightening fate that befell William. How was Paul capable of pursuing issues that seemed lethal to William? Though frail of body since childhood, he was not frail of mind.

The narrator makes it known that Paul was a master of observation from the very beginning of his life. The capacity to observe buffered him to some extent from the toxicity of his mother. What he observed was catastrophic but the fact that he could observe at all was a source of redemption. Paul was capable of observation. William was not. The very fact that Paul could observe, though from a standpoint of passivity, enabled him to develop a conflict-free sphere of his ego. He was motivated to paint and honed his craft to become an accomplished artist. Though Gertrude Morel intruded into most aspects of her children's lives, she left Paul alone when it came to painting. As a result, Paul was able to eke out an experience of autonomy through artistic expression. His mother was limited to valuing only the prizes he won for his paintings, appropriating his accomplishments as hers. She never actually valued the paintings themselves and was not clever enough to realize that Paul had gravitated to emotional turf that she had no interest in dominating. In this way, Paul made initial strides towards emotional separation from his mother. To his detriment, they only amounted to initial strides and not the full experience of autonomy. He was unable to understand no less overcome his anguish. The novel ends with Paul's gut-wrenching grief over the death of his mother. Her death left him unattached and existentially lost. Tormented by the prospect of being incapable of surviving it, he ultimately chose to walk into the night towards the lights of the town. Herein lies a glimpse of hope that he might begin to form a life of his own. His fate at the end of the novel is tenuous and uncertain.

* * *

The emotional injury

Aspects of the emotional injury suffered by the narcissistically wounded child have been addressed in the last chapter. Alienation from one's feelings and self, domination by a superior power and abject misery are the primary dimensions of this condition. What remains to gather is a deepening of the awareness of the dynamics by considering the ways in which development goes awry. Specifically, it is important to unravel the impact of this injury on adolescence and young adulthood. *Sons and Lovers* focuses on Paul's life in adolescence and emerging adulthood. Emotional injury is revealed through Paul's inner experience at this developmental stage.

To set the context for grasping the vicissitudes of experience at adolescence, it is instructive to turn to the work of Peter Blos. In *The Second Individuation of Adolescence*, Blos offers an enormous contribution to psychoanalytic developmental thought by describing the process of the restructuring of the mind at adolescence (Blos, 1967, pp. 162–186). He contends that the momentum of psychic energy at puberty drives the adolescent in normal development to regress to an earlier stage. This regression is a developmental requirement rather than a defense. The aim of this regression is to revisit infantile dependencies, loosen infantile object ties and free psychic energy for the formation of new relationships. By modifying superego constraints, this process enables the adolescent to reclaim psychic energy for the investment in an ego ideal. In so doing, maturation (both physically and psychically) is advanced for the consolidation of identity and the capacity to assume personal responsibility. Identity formation confirms the adolescent as a unique individual creating his own life.

Blos builds on the developmental model of separation–individuation set out by Mahler. For Mahler and Blos, the structuring of the mind through this process occurs at a time of heightened vulnerability of personality organization. Blos states "the profoundest and most unique quality of adolescence lies in its capacity to move between regressive and progressive consciousness with an ease that has no equal at any other period in human life" (Blos, 1967, p. 178). The second individuation presents the adolescent with a second opportunity at managing danger situations of childhood. One can appreciate how tenuous adolescent development can be in the face of this regressive pull. It is amazing that any adolescent emerges intact into young adulthood. In terms of the narcissistic drama, the derailment of the second individuation process resulting in failure of individuation is the source of concern.

In *Sons and Lovers*, Paul's misery is largely due to his inability and unwillingness to shed his emotional dependency on his mother. This inability is based on the fact that his mother did everything in her power to thwart his emotional emancipation. He was raised with a sense of ambivalence about the prospect of individuation. This ambivalence is witnessed in his agonizing reflections over failed attempts at intimacy as an adolescent. Though he is drawn to Miriam he cannot have an intimate relationship with her. Paul is tortured both by his mother's voiced disapproval and by appearing disloyal to the archaic toxic maternal introject. When enveloped by the negative side of this ambivalence, Paul frequently feels genuine hatred for

Miriam. This hatred is due to an over-identification with the toxic introject. Clara, one of the least astute characters in the novel, realizes that Paul is blind to the fact that Miriam's love for him is genuine. Paul's dependence on his mother obstructs his capacity to form nurturing relationships. It is the lack of individuation that stuns him at the end of the novel. Who is he? What is his identity? What does he stand for? Who is truly part of his life? These are the kinds of questions that torment him. The origin of his predicament boils down to the actions of the unconscious assassin.

Paul's interest in Clara does not threaten his mother. It also represents a failure at individuation. As an older woman who has long estranged herself from her husband, Clara is the spitting image of Gertrude Morel. Rather than exploring new relationships (that is, with Miriam), Paul reaffirms infantile object ties through his involvement with Clara. This relationship, though consummated sexually, ultimately fades away. Paul becomes bored with Clara and aware of the lack of true intimacy with her. In the end, Paul lacks both a parental ideal and an ego ideal.

It is important to note Blos' observation about the nature of conscience or superego at the second individuation. In healthy development, psychic energy at adolescence is freed from early objects to become invested in new relationships, the ego ideal and the transformation of the superego from critic to guide. The primitive critical superego gives way to one that provides guidance about judgment and choices. What is important about this distinction is that the primitive superego engenders a sense of guilt while the superego at adolescence allows for learning experiences. The manner in which conscience manifests in Paul Morel is yet another indication of the depth of his emotional injury. His self-reflection is riddled with self flagellation.

* * *

The death of Gertrude Morel

At the end of *Sons and Lovers*, Mrs. Morel falls mortally ill with cancer. There is nothing medically that can be done for her. She wants to die. She is confined to her room, bedridden, taking medication for the pain. Paul is thrown into turmoil by his mother's decline and impending demise. On a conscious level, he cannot bear to witness her pain. He desperately wants her death to be merciful rather than painful. Her dying takes much longer than Paul can bear. He is tortured by the sound of her shallow breaths. Finally she dies.

It is known from biographical material that D. H. Lawrence himself endured this very experience with his mother. Lawrence turned towards literature to attend to his feelings about his mother's death and the earth-shattering impact it had on him. Paul's plunge into a state of being utterly lost upon his mother's death is what our narcissistically injured patients report as their experience when object loss occurs quickly and drastically. The concurrent formation of new relationships can ease the blow. One resource in this regard is analytic group psychotherapy.

Matricides bring to mind the plot in Alfred Hitchcock's classic thriller, *Psycho*. The psychiatrist's summation at the end of the film explains that the protagonist, Norman Bates, murdered his mother in a jealous rage. Norman Bates was an only child raised by his mother. His father died when he was five years old. Norman's mother is described as clinging and highly demanding. One can readily discern that she was severely narcissistic. The obstruction of Norman's process of emotional separation is axiomatic under these circumstances.

The clinical outcome in the case of Norman Bates is clearly more extreme than that of Paul Morel. Norman Bates becomes psychotic and therein resides the tension and anxiety induced by the film. The psychiatrist explains that Norman's symbiotic relationship with his mother resulted in installing her image in his mind as, what I call, the toxic maternal introject. It is this introject that led him to poison his mother and her gentleman friend ten years prior to the dramatic action in the film. Norman could not tolerate any interference with this symbiotic relationship. He killed his mother and her suitor in a jealous rage. Norman then carried on in psychosis with his mother very much alive in his mind. He exhumed her body and hallucinated that she lived with him in their old Victorian home above the Bates Motel. Her shrill, caustic voice resounded in his mind. The murder of Marion in the now famous shower scene was also enacted by the toxic introject in a jealous rage. Norman was sexually attracted to her. The introject arranged for the murder of Marion to preserve the symbiosis. The psychiatrist notes that Norman Bates, once apprehended by the police, no longer exists. He eerily indicated that Norman's mother as the toxic introject finally engulfed him completely. The camera zooms in on Norman, sitting alone in the prison cell wrapped in a blanket, speaking to himself in his mother's voice.

Hitchcock delves into the peril of thwarted emotional separation on an unconscious level. His metaphor for the unconscious lies in situating the Bates Motel off the beaten track. Early in the film, Norman mentions that, ever since the interstate highway was built several years before, no one comes to the Bates Motel without having lost his way. In *Psycho*, Hitchcock explores an arena of experience that is normally kept from conscious awareness. He never intended for the actual murders to be what is most frightening about the film. While both murders occur by stabbing with a large knife, Hitchcock resisted diverting attention by staging a great deal of blood and gore as one might expect by today's standards. Rather, he leads the viewer to the real source of terror in the film—namely, the unspeakable violence experienced in adults who as children were prevented from separating from the narcissistic mother. The murderous rage in the child is in direct proportion to the hatred foisted upon it by the unconscious assassin. It is this violent reaction to emotional blackmail that drives the child towards murderous fury. It is into this abyss of fear of violent impulses that Hitchcock wants the viewer to plunge. The immediacy of film itself and Hitchcock's genius deprive the viewer of the opportunity to marshal defenses quickly enough against the recognition of a sudden surge of murderous retribution.

Hitchcock's explicit message about murderous rage is what underlies Paul's repressed aggression towards his engulfing mother. While feelings of hatred openly pervade *Sons and Lovers*, this sense of retributive murderous rage is muted throughout. What is witnessed instead, is the profound fallout on certain characters. In this respect, one needs only to consider the death of William and Paul's agonizing attack on his own mind.

CHAPTER FOUR

The way out

The Archimedean point

In unveiling possible routes to psychological freedom from the clutches of the unconscious assassin, it is necessary first to identify the goal that is the destination of this journey. Sufficient attention has been paid to the psychologically oppressive effects of the narcissistic drama on the development of the targeted child. The sense of psychological freedom in this context consists both of "freedom from" (that is, oppression) and "freedom to" (that is, the pursuit of happiness). As of the end of *Sons and Lovers*, Paul Morel is existentially lost in the wake of his mother's death. With this catastrophic loss, he confronts the possibility of being released both from her direct domination and his need to be dominated by her. It leaves him groundless and full of *Angst* in the Heideggerian sense (Heidegger, 1927, p. 393). The association to Heidegger's conception of *Angst* is apt as witnessed in Paul's experience of collapsing into himself and confronting his own most non-existence. He endures tormenting suffering that gives way to a capacity to summon the courage to carry on and live. The image is, at the end, one of Paul staggering in bewilderment at night towards the lights of the town. While this description provides a glimpse into a first affirmation of life on his own terms, one is left witnessing Paul in crisis without resolution. As the novel ends, there is no indication of where Paul might end up in life or what kind of person he might become. This ending signifies both an end to Paul's emotional suffering at the hands of his mother and an allusion to a new beginning. From a psychological point of view, what might this new beginning be? What is the direction in which those of us identifying with Paul are heading? In my view, the goal is ultimately to have and value a life of one's own. The centerpiece of that life is the autonomous pursuit of happiness. Adults can attain it through various possible routes at the appropriate stages in the life cycle. It serves as the potential for positive resolution of Erikson's epigenetic stages of intimacy *vs.* isolation, generativity *vs.* self-absorption and integrity *vs.* despair (Erikson, 1959, p. 129). Ideally, the goal is to achieve the highest possible quality of life in both work and love. Therefore, this odyssey that navigates around exploitation, domination, and hatred is aimed at gravitating towards work that is self-affirming and love that is reciprocal. This is the birthright of being a person.

Having laid out this goal, it is time to turn our attention to ways of attaining it. Lifting oneself out of the depressive morass of the narcissistic drama is a major focus of this book. It is the principal concern of all narcissistically injured patients. The capacities necessary to entertain possible routes out of this crisis include awareness of psychic pain, curiosity as to its origin, and the incentive to understand and do something about it. How does one get the unconscious assassin out of one's head? This question compounds the experience of exasperation, frustration, confusion, and even agony. There might even be a fantasy to remove the unconscious assassin surgically, if it were at all possible. Many suffer alone in self-doubt and hopelessness. They are at a loss about whether anyone can understand and empathize with them. Feelings of shame augment this sense of isolation. The silent misery either impels one towards seeking emotional support and contemplating a search for alternatives or leaves one sunken ever inward towards despair and resignation.

In *The Drama of the Gifted Child*, Alice Miller adroitly addresses the origin and dynamics of the narcissistic drama. She provides clinical vignettes as a useful tool to demonstrate the evolution of personality disturbance arising from emotional injury in childhood. Many have gained awareness of their emotional plight from her book but express disappointment that it does not specifically address the issue of emotional resolution of their injuries. While Miller implies the need for psychoanalytic psychotherapy to treat these conditions, it became apparent that there is a felt need for an explicit discussion of paths towards achieving psychic healing. That effort is pursued here.

It is astonishing that any person emotionally damaged by the narcissistic drama might be capable of prevailing over enormous odds to lead a productively autonomous life. It is a testament to the human spirit that this resilience ever occurs. Whatever psychological developmental explanations are given to account for it, the truth is that it remains essentially a mystery in the sense conveyed by Gabriel Marcel (Marcel, 1956, pp. 9–46).

The ancient Greek mathematician, Archimedes, allegedly maintained that he would be able to move the earth with a fulcrum and a lever of sufficient length. It was the seventeenth-century philosopher, Descartes, who formulated the "cogito" as his Archimedean point of certainty. It served as the foundation for his system of knowledge. There is an Archimedean point of certainty involved in lifting oneself out of the abyss of the narcissistic drama. It consists of an awareness of abject misery, a desire to know one's true self and an urge to do something about it. There is a multitude of ways to pursue psychological freedom and prominent ones are addressed in the following discussion.

* * *

Creativity and risk

The cumulative psychic energy of frustration, fear and outrage due to the narcissistic drama can impel one towards self-expression in a variety of ways. One major channel for this energy is through engaging in creativity. From a psychoanalytic point of view, creativity offers the possibility of sublimation of psychic tension in conflict-free spheres of functioning. By creativity, I am referring to making art—whether it is painting, music, sculpture, literature, poetry, dance, etc. While a work of art is an entity in itself resting on its own merit, the very process of creativity confers special meaning for the artist in coming to terms with emotional suffering. Rather than being consumed by this suffering, which may have its own inevitability in the end, the artist makes an effort to express it, to get it out, to observe it as an idiosyncratic formulation. The work of art itself is not aimed necessarily at providing an answer to any particular problem. Rather, it is an authentic representation of vital experience in the medium chosen by the artist. It presupposes that the artist's capacity for creativity has not been crushed by an arbitrary or superior force. In other words, the artist is free to create art. The creative drive is not extinguished by either external oppression or internal repression. In addition, the artist demonstrates a willingness to assume the risks involved in self-expression. These features instill a sense of liberation in an artist.

It is constructive and useful to consider prominent examples of artistic expression under the duress of the narcissistic drama. One that is readily at hand is D. H. Lawrence himself.

He wrote *Sons and Lovers* as an autobiographical endeavor. While the novel stands on its own as a work of art, it is clear that Lawrence engaged in examining his life through literary creativity for some good reason. In my review of the literature, I did not come across any documentation that Lawrence ever explicitly revealed the impetus for writing this novel. He completed it in 1913 at the age of twenty-eight. The novel itself ends when Paul Morel, with whom Lawrence identifies, is twenty-four years old. It seems reasonable to assume then, that Lawrence applied his considerable literary gifts to reviewing, observing, and describing the vicissitudes of his life as a young man.

So, why did Lawrence write *Sons and Lovers* in the first place? Only Lawrence himself could answer that question. However, from a psychological point of view, it is interesting to speculate about certain possible explanations. One obvious possibility is that Lawrence struggled to make sense of his own emotional pain and awkwardness. Paul's perpetual ruminations suggest this notion. There is also the possibility that he intended to show the world how his narcissistic mother oppressed him. In the same way that Mrs. Morel did not crush Paul's artistic expression as a painter, Lawrence's mother did not disable him from becoming a writer. For Lawrence, creative writing could have represented an outlet through which his psychic torment could be mediated. There is also the specific matter of his involvement in his mother's death. As a major emotional upheaval for Paul in the novel, it reflects Lawrence's suffering in this respect as well. One can only imagine the enormous and complex feelings of guilt that Lawrence must have experienced in carrying out his mother's mercy killing. As a pivotal experience in his life, it makes perfect sense that he would be impelled to write about it. Among the purposes that it might serve are confession, self-judgment and confronting guilt.

The historical context of the publishing of *Sons and Lovers* is relevant as well. It was in 1900 that Freud introduced *The*

Interpretation of Dreams, ushering in a revolutionary new understanding of the human mind. Lawrence came of age intellectually at this time and eventually gravitated towards the works of Carl Jung. The tenor of *Sons and Lovers* reflects Lawrence's exposure to and appreciation of depth psychology. The emphasis of the novel is on the phenomenological portrayal of experience itself rather than towards any theoretical working through of that experience. It is for this primary reason that the novel was selected as the clinical material utilized for this book.

A more modern example of this kind of creative self-expression can be found in the life of Paddy Chayevsky. He wrote screenplays for television and film that spanned the 1950s into the early 1980s. He is the only person to have received Oscars for screenplays for three films—*Marty* (1955), *The Hospital* (1971) and *Network* (1976). However, most of his screenplays were not commercial successes. Chayevsky was known to have been a ruthless social commentator ahead of his time (Considine, 2000). From piercing sensitivity about being a social outcast in *Marty* to satirical dismantling of the television industry in *Network*, Chayevsky unnerved audiences with scathing portrayals of the sacred ground of everyday life. He prided himself on originality and used film and television to pursue autobiographical themes.

A brief survey of his biography demonstrates how the narcissistic drama played out in his life. The last of three sons, he was born in this country to Russian Jewish immigrants. His father was a successful businessman and raised his family in the Bronx. Both of his parents took an active interest in his intellectual and musical development. While his father's interest in him was joyful and nurturing, his mother on the other hand was demanding and exacting. She forced him to excel at piano, ordering him to relentlessly practice for many grueling hours at a time. His resentment towards his tyrannical mother and, by extension, classical piano evolved into rage. As an adult, he sublimated this rage into his writing.

Though born with the name, Sydney, and bound to orthodox Jewish tenets, he adopted the name, Paddy, in the army and abandoned his religious observance. While his rage was constrained and repressed as "Sydney", the new identity of "Paddy" gave him license to say anything he wanted to say. The entirety of his writing is a scathing criticism of the country that his mother revered through her experience of assimilation. In other words, it is a displacement. In tearing down the social fabric and hypocrisies of American society, Chayevsky was tearing down his mother's idealizations, and he did it with zeal and relish. Chayevsky's words screamed by Peter Finney at the end of *Network* are a virtual anthem for every child oppressed by an unconscious assassin: "I'm mad as hell and I'm not taking it anymore!" (Chayevesky, 1976).

There are countless ways out of this dilemma that are not associated with creativity per se. Chayevsky's anthem in the political sphere leads to a life of activism. As noted earlier in the discussion of Adrienne Rich, political activism is likely the most direct way of focusing on the abuses of power in the narcissistic dilemma as they manifest in terms of society and the world. As it happens, some of the closest people in my life are political activists whose early lives happened to have been tinged by the realities of their own narcissistic drama. They ultimately developed an acute awareness of the imbalance of power as a political rather than a psychological phenomenon. This observation does not in any way diminish the inherent value of the moral underpinnings of their mission. Activists are doers. By definition, they engage in purposeful action to bring about constructive socio-political change. For them, understanding the dynamics of power is as second nature as breathing itself. From their point of view, psychological explanations may sometimes be seen as irrelevant or even subversive. My discussions with them usually end with the acknowledgement that there is a place for exploring ideas in the course of changing the world.

* * *

Psychotherapy

Having made the case that there are many types of exit strategies from the narcissistic drama, it is now necessary to elucidate the one approach that distinguishes itself by providing transparency with regard to the emotional injury and process of healing. That approach is psychotherapy in general and psychoanalytic psychotherapy in particular.

The benefit of psychotherapy, broadly speaking, is to offer a forum for exploration of thoughts and feelings about emotional wounds and the possibility of healing them. It is transparent in the sense that emotional injury is embedded in a framework of understanding the nature of the mind and how it develops. In taking the experience of psychic pain directly and thematically, it diverges from the route of sublimation through creativity as just observed.

Psychotherapy is not merely a form of treatment. More importantly, it facilitates progressive emotional growth. Ultimately, it is a learning experience that has nothing to do with formal education. It is a process of learning about oneself on an emotional level pertaining to the entire spectrum of experience. It is a tool in one's quest to identify what counts as fulfillment in life. Learning in this way takes time. It involves the activity of the mind in reformulating itself by virtue of new discoveries and perspectives. There is constant interaction between the individual in psychotherapy and the process of psychotherapy itself. As a result, both are constantly being influenced by each other. The outcome over time is an increasingly informed patient taking an active role in shaping a progressively deeper experience of psychotherapy. This is what is meant by the word "progressive" in describing successful treatment.

As previously stated, this process of self-discovery begins in awareness of not being good enough and an urge to search into why one might feel this way. At first, the courage to disclose one's emotional pain to a college counselor, teacher, nurse, etc. constitutes the initial step. Usually, it is experienced as an enormous emotional risk to initiate disclosure of personal problems tinged with shame and vulnerability. The great value of taking this first step cannot be overstated because it sets the stage for taking many such steps to follow. Conveying one's emotional pain in confidence and desperate need to a reliable and responsible other person is the Archimedean point for beginning to take charge of one's own feelings and life.

Having established this point, one then meanders among helpful and less helpful people to become better informed about the kind of psychotherapist or psychotherapists who are best suited to forming a working relationship. This is the nature of the search and it falls completely upon one's own shoulders. Over time, one discovers better therapeutic matches. The point here is not that one's search necessarily involves interminable psychotherapy and successive therapists. It is to say that, over time, one's intuition about choosing a psychotherapist becomes more refined based on experience. Disappointments in the choice of therapists along the way can be encountered as part of the learning process. For this reason, one must take an active rather than passive role in the process. Periodic evaluation of the quality of the progress in any treatment is appropriate and recommended. It is my clinical view that the indications for any treatment should be driven by the patient's emotional state of need and advancement in the context of consensus with the psychotherapist. Many decide that more than one experience of psychotherapy is beneficial.

Admiration and respect for a person's meandering constructive path towards emotional relief and maturation are core values. This attitude is reflected in the writings of D. W. Winnicott. He called attention to the process in which emotionally burdened patients brought themselves to his office and regularly attended sessions for long periods of time before they could actually engage in the therapeutic process itself. Winnicott described these individuals as having a "caretaker self" whose role it was to bring the patient's "true self" to the therapeutic setting (Winnicott, 1960, p. 142). Winnicott, in this case, was acutely sensitive to the moment when the process of psychotherapy would actually begin—and it is clearly not always coincident with the patient first appearing in the office. It is the caretaker self that conducts the search for the therapist and paves the way by ascertaining emotional safety for the "true self" to emerge.

So, the path towards therapeutic progress can be one of fits and starts, disappointments, or even a sense of wasting time. The aim, of course, is to promote emotional growth itself and it is achieved through perseverance.

This is not the place to take up a discussion of or comparisons among various schools of thought in psychotherapy. While it may be of interest to some, it is viewed, in this context, as a diversion from the aim of this book—and that aim has been to pursue the original question: How does the child of a severely narcissistic mother emerge to become an autonomous adult? And that question is embedded in the theory of developmental psychoanalytic psychotherapy.

* * *

Therapeutic action

Having established that the most transparent way out of the narcissistic drama is psychoanalytic psychotherapy, the question remains as to how psychic relief or cure is accomplished. The term used to describe what is curative is therapeutic action.

It encompasses what is actually done in the dynamic between patient and therapist to lift misery and advance emotional growth. Another formulation for emotional growth is the term structural change—that is, change in aspects of the functioning of the mind that promote emotional development. It stands to reason that if the primitive dyad (between the mother and infant) was the original source of the developmental conflict and injury, then the resolution sought in adulthood must occur within a new dyad (therapist and patient). Loewald introduced his thoughts on therapeutic action with the following observation: "If structural changes in the patient's personality means anything, it must mean that ego-development is resumed in the therapeutic process of psycho-analysis. And this resumption of ego-development is contingent on the relationship with the new object, the analyst" (Loewald, 1960, p. 20). He then proceeded to state:

> I have said that the analyst, through interpretations of transference distortions, increasingly becomes available to the patient as a new object. And this not primarily in the sense of an object previously met, but the newness consists in the patient's rediscovery of early paths of the development of object-relations leading to a new way of relating to objects and of being oneself. (Loewald, 1960, p. 20)

Loewald illuminated the point that the therapeutic relationship in the new dyad has the potential to activate core emotional conflict in order to provide an opportunity for resolution. It thereby offers an appropriate forum with specificity to bring about healing. According to Loewald, "The patient, in order to attain structural changes in his ego-organization, needs the relatedness with a consistently mature object" (Loewald, 1960, p. 20). In other words, in order to conduct and support the treatment, the therapist must have a higher level of ego-organization than the patient. Moreover, the consistency of this higher level of organization is crucial in neutralizing the inconsistency and damage inflicted by the archaic mother.

It is not difficult to accept that the therapeutic relationship as the new dyad is charged with revisiting and resolving emotional injury sustained within the original dyad. The real challenge consists both in conceiving the possibility of resolution and describing the dynamics of the process by which it is achieved. One major impetus in writing this book has been to meet this task in a way that is intelligible and accessible to people in general and not just to those in the field familiar with psychological jargon. While this is a necessary and noble goal, it abounds with significant complications. The principal complication is language itself.

The dynamics of psychotherapy occur in the emotional sphere. The primary phenomena are on an experiential level—namely, the experience of emotions as well as the action of emotions. Language is an abstraction from the primary phenomena of experience. It is used to convey information from one mind to another about the nature of primary phenomena. Language is not the phenomena itself. The reason for this concern about language is based on the high premium at work here in terms of providing the most pristine rendering possible of experience itself. When considering what actually constitutes the healing process in psychotherapy, the burden of explanation lies in the limitations of language itself. At best, descriptive language aimed at careful approximation of experience is what is obtainable. Even with the most painstaking effort to minimize jargon and use neutral language, it is unavoidable to encounter theoretical underpinnings and the hidden meaning of words. Rather than admit futility and abandon the entire project, it is important to read the description of the healing process as an imperfect rendering of the emotional dynamics themselves.

It was in this vein that Lawrence's *Sons and Lovers* was chosen as the clinical material for my views in this book. In the novel, Lawrence has provided a phenomenology of experience from the narrator's point of view and pertaining, for the most part, to the thoughts and feelings of Paul Morel. The choice of this material substantiates the value placed on primary experience itself. This value is based on the knowledge obtained by getting as close to actual experience as possible, and it is this very knowledge that is imparted here to advance the understanding of how psychotherapy heals.

A final observation about the paradox of language as laying bare experience itself can be witnessed in the philosophy of Martin Heidegger. His seminal work and perhaps the most significant philosophical text of the twentieth century, *Being and Time*, is an endeavor to uncover the nature of Being or Truth by analyzing the being of human being. In his rigorous effort at grasping the pristine nature of human being, he develops neologisms and a language saturated in jargon that can only be seen as opaque to readers without a philosophical background. For instance, human being is characterized ontologically by the German term "Da-sein" or being-there (Heidegger, 1927, p. 38). In other words, Heidegger's most pristine rendering of human being is as "being there". What does it mean to have perhaps the most brilliant description of human being inaccessible to people in general? First, it means that there is nothing simple about fundamental principles and ideas. What appears at first to be a straightforward matter, such as the definition of a human being, is ultimately embedded in a vast complexity of knowledge-seeking in general. Second, language becomes conflated and utterly inadequate the closer one comes to approximating experience itself. It is a kind of linguistic Heisenberg uncertainty principle. Alfred Hitchcock had the perspicacity to realize that film is a medium with closer access to emotional experience than language. Music as well appeals more readily to the emotions than spoken language. By "language" I am clearly referring to discursive language. Poetry and performance art would fall more into the category with film and music. The advantage that film and music have over discursive language when it comes to tapping primary experience is the quality of immediacy. Language mediates experience through cognition and so represents a layer of abstraction.

What is therapeutic action? It is actually many things. According to Loewald, it is concretely the dynamic activity of bringing about psychic healing or structural change in treatment. It is also the title of Jonathan Lear's brilliant and remarkable book on the same subject. Lear's book, *Therapeutic Action*, is taken up with a careful reading of Loewald's central paper on the nature of therapeutic action. Together, Loewald and Lear provide a glimpse into the actual workings of the process of emotional repair in treatment. They advance Freud's general notion of treatment as "working through" emotional conflict through free association by elucidating the specific prospects of the process by which healing is accomplished. To my mind, this accomplishment is outstanding. It needs to be presented in a manner that is within the reach of people in general. It should be stated parenthetically that Lear knew Loewald personally towards the end of his life. Conversations that Lear had with Loewald inform his book.

Therapeutic action for Lear goes beyond the actual healing dynamic of treatment. To read and reread *Therapeutic Action* is to be engaged fully and fundamentally in what it means to be a psychotherapist, how to think about psychotherapy and to consider the value that underlies the entire endeavor. Technically, Lear writes about psychoanalysts, a certain kind of psychotherapist. Psychoanalysts submit to extensive training and practice in accordance with the tenets of psychoanalysis as conceived by Freud. With due respect for Lear's project, it is my view that his comments about psychoanalysts can be extended as well to include psychoanalytic psychotherapists. The call in Lear's book is a call for aliveness—that is, our aliveness as therapists, aliveness in the process of treatment and the requirement of sustaining authentic openness as possible from moment to moment. According to Lear, the identity of a therapist pertains less to actual function but more to who we essentially are. Lear states that:

> this process of continually coming back to ourselves as psychoanalysts is itself part of therapeutic action ... As psychoanalysts, we begin our training with our own analysis. We hope that the therapeutic action of that analysis enabled us eventually to get up from the couch and continue on as analysts. For therapeutic action does not describe a process, like getting a tattoo, which has an end point. Once you've gotten a tattoo, you've got a tattoo; indeed, once you've had an analysis, you've had an analysis, but therapeutic action goes on and on. Analysis has a termination, therapeutic action does not. Ideally, one continues one's own process of therapeutic action as a lifetime project. As an analyst, this process is lived out in the myriad activities of facilitating therapeutic action in others. (Lear, 2003, p. 33)

Lear's point is that being a therapist consists of the ongoing process of becoming a therapist. The diploma on the wall is not what confirms the identity of a therapist as a therapist. Rather, it is the continual reshaping of therapists as therapists that substantiates the identity.

Ultimately, being is becoming. Lear's call is for keeping the flame of aliveness in terms of honesty, newness, and openness constantly lit. This notion is reminiscent of Socrates' quest for knowledge through questioning that pervades the Platonic dialogues. Philosophizing is not a static state. Socrates engaged in philosophy out a continual need for examination of himself and others as part of being alive. Therefore, becoming a therapist is an endless project in the same respect that Socratic philosophizing is endless. It has to do with the nature of human being as incomplete and the fact that human beings are not omniscient. This sense of incompleteness or being at a loss is captured by the Greek word, "aporia", in Plato's *Apology*. It is due to aporia that one is impelled towards a constant sense of renewal. In the end, aporia characterizes us as therapists in the process of ever becoming therapists.

Lear shares the concern over the difficulty in maintaining this sense of aliveness in writing about and discussing therapeutic action.

> The terms with which we communicate, no matter what they are—'unconscious' or 'ego' or 'intersubjectivity' or 'object relations' or 'bad breast' or 'play of signifiers'— tend to lose their vibrancy as they are passed along in the community. This is the entropy of thought: Whatever life the concepts might have had when they are first being applied in vivid psychoanalytic contexts tends to get drained out of them, and they get turned more and more into slogans. Eventually, the terms get used in place of thinking rather that as an expression of it. The ultimate absurdity is a dead paper on therapeutic action. The entropy of thought is not a problem that can be completely avoided. It is endemic to thinking itself. Even the phrase 'entropy of thought' can become a cliché. So too can warnings about it. So, the task is to bring our concepts to life. (Lear, 2003, p. 34)

Lear is exhorting us to advance and preserve a sense of vitality in thinking about and discussing psychotherapy. It is not simply a high standard towards which we should aspire. It is the only standard aiming at authenticity.

Lear's *Therapeutic Action* stands out as the most explicit effort to describe how psychological freedom is attained through treatment. It is the most straightforward, though by no means simple rendering of how psychotherapy can be therapeutic. The task here is to attempt to describe the hallmarks of this healing process in a way that is directly within reach of people in general and, so, available for their lives. It is not intended to be a substitute for reading *Therapeutic Action*. For this psychotherapist, studying *Therapeutic Action* has been life-altering.

The therapeutic project taken up here is the neutralization or even possible eradication of the unconscious assassin. In treatment, the therapist is attentive to the patient's unconscious processing and material. As Freud instructed, the ultimate aim is to make the unconscious conscious. How this is done is the art of therapy. It is important to appreciate that, both within a particular treatment and regarding treatments cumulatively over time, the process of bringing the unconscious assassin to consciousness can be slow and arduous. There is no indication in *Sons and Lovers* that Paul Morel ever wondered about harboring an unconscious assassin in the depths of his mind. It is not until the very end of the novel, with the death of his mother and his subsequent existential crisis, that he appears remotely open to consider it as a possibility. The ultimate question remains as to how to neutralize the toxic and even lethal effects of the unconscious assassin in order to set the stage for attaining psychological freedom. Another formulation of this point is to put the ghost of the unconscious assassin to rest once and for all.

One may recall Loewald maintained that, for structural change to occur, the patient requires a consistently mature object in the form of the therapist. Both Loewald and Lear refer to the differential in maturity levels between the patient and therapist as the differential between a lower level of organization and a higher level, respectively. This does not mean that the therapist is superior as a person to the patient. What it means is that the therapist has the capacity to orient the treatment in such a way as to enable the patient to regress to early developmental stages at which the original narcissistic injury took place. Loewald explains that this regression is not defensive but occurs in the service of the ego as a requirement for the resumption of ego-development (Loewald, 1960, pp. 24–25). It is in the context of this regression that the therapist intervenes to promote the patient's effort to bring previously unconscious material in the preconscious to consciousness. Therefore, this regression sets the stage for the possibility of psychic healing.

Regression in the service of the ego for the patient is made possible by the phenomenon of transference. Transference and resistance are core Freudian concepts. Transference basically consists of the phenomenon of displacing feelings and fantasies towards important figures in the patient's early life onto the therapist. For the most part, resistance constitutes defensive measures against anxiety in the face of conflict (Blanck & Blanck, 1974). Lear's depiction of transference is especially elegant. He states the following:

> Now what is striking about this transference is not merely the particular role I am assigned, but that I am assigned a role that sustains a world. It is not simply that I am another disappointing figure, but I secure the world as disappointing. (Lear, 2003, pp. 203–204)

Lear's concept of "world" or "worldhood" is taken from Heidegger's conception of human being as "Dasein". "Worldhood" lies within "Dasein" as being-in-the-world. What the patient does through transference is not simply paste categories of "father" or "mother" onto the therapist, The phenomenon is far more profound than that. The truth is that, through transference and regression, the patient invites the therapist into his or her own world itself—that is, the very world in which emotional derailment originally took place resulting in narcissistic injury. This invitation occurs on both conscious and unconscious levels. There is an unconscious wish for corrective relatedness to promote emotional growth. The invitation enables the patient to summon the therapist to a place of high vulnerability and psychic charge for the sake of having a new and reparative experience of the injury itself. It is precisely this new experience that brings about structural change and the resumption of ego-development.

Lear offers a humorous and illuminating description of how transference rears its head in treatment. He notes that:

> The figures are not only coming from the past, they are coming from an earlier type of world-formation. Imagine them emerging from, say, an acquatic world. Analyst and analysand are on a dinghy, neither really knows the seas. For a while you just sit in the dinghy and drift along; then, wonk! A huge tentacle whacks the boat and fastens to the side. With associations and interpretations one can follow the tentacle down a bit; but then, wonk! Another tentacle hits the other side. One continues this way until an octopus is suddenly hugging the boat. This is the transference neurosis. A good analyst is like a fisherman: he knows that if he waits with analytic patience, the octopus will eventually be clamoring to get on deck. (Lear, 2003, pp. 206–207)

Once the transference has been established and the therapist has been invited into the patient's world by virtue of the patient's regression, the therapist must intervene to shape the possibility for structural change. Two major questions arise: First, what counts as structural change in the patient? And, second, by what means does the therapist facilitate this change? The answer to the first question is complex and can be approached in the following way. The therapist facilitates the patient's overall effort to bring unconscious conflict and material into consciousness. Unconscious conflict involving the unconscious assassin seeps into the patient's preconscious sphere through associations and interpretations. There, it is accessible to probing by the conscious ego, which then lifts the material into consciousness. The therapist's actual action will be detailed in a moment.

Once the conflict reaches consciousness, ego-development can resume with the support and guidance of the therapist. In so doing, the patient is able to gain a new experience of the original injury within the emotional safety of the new dyad. This process constitutes healing within the patient's psyche through integration of the old in terms of the new. This integration is itself a central part of structural change. The enormous amount of psychic energy formerly bound up in primitive intrapsychic defenses can then be liberated for emotional growth and the pursuit of the ego ideal. Structural change is evidenced by the ego's newfound capacity to energize the ego ideal. The net effect is for the ego to become psychologically unburdened by the unconscious assassin and free to become spontaneously involved and invested in the world. In its entirely, this is a process of reclaiming aliveness.

Lear provides a unique and brilliantly effective portrayal of how the therapist actually goes about facilitating structural change in the patient. The approach that he adopts is one of irony. I will not attempt either to define "irony" here or to present what Lear means by it. What is indispensable in this regard is to read *Therapeutic Action* itself to learn about the nature of irony and how Lear makes use of it in treatment. As Lear himself points out in introducing this concept, the definition in the dictionary is utterly inadequate in characterizing such a nuanced and profound term (Lear, 2003, pp. 65–66). It is the meaning of irony found in the words of Socrates as written by Plato and in the writings of Kierkegaard. Suffice it to say that irony here relates to deep understanding of what it means to be human and to carefully apprehend experience itself. Socratic irony is captured in his claim to ignorance in the face of the pronouncement by the Oracle of Delphi that he is the wisest of all. This is how irony works according to Lear: "the act of becoming ironic is an act of unifying the psyche"

(Lear, 2003, pp. 176–177). It is precisely the exchange of irony between therapist and patient that stimulates the capacity in the patient to integrate past and present to achieve a newly uplifted experience of the original injury. The depth of this process can readily be grasped. It is through associations generated by irony that the patient is able to retrieve preconscious material into consciousness. For the first time, the patient's ego is able to experience the unconscious assassin for what it is and strive to put it to rest. This is the epitome of the healing process from the narcissistic drama.

* * *

Being in the moment

A word needs to be said about how the therapist actually participates in therapeutic action through irony. The transference and requisite regression set the stage for what I refer to as the affective moment of structural change. It is the patient's invitation to the therapist that makes this convergence possible. Recall that the therapist's world involves a higher level of ego-organization relative to the patient's. It is precisely this convergence of the two worlds in the course of treatment that, including a momentary alteration in the experience of time, makes healing through structural change achievable.

The experience of time is altered in this affectively charged moment because past, present, and future cohere simultaneously. From the standpoint of his fundamental ontology, Heidegger views linear time as artifact or "*ontic*". For human being in its essence, that is authentic "Dasein", Heidegger devises the term "temporality". Temporality represents the authentic experience of time and is basically yet another formulation for Dasein. Heidegger arrives at the following seminal statement: "Temporality temporalizes itself as a future making present in the process of having been" (Heidegger,

1927, p. 401). Heidegger's point here bears out our conclusion that this affective moment of emotional growth captures the essence of what we are as human beings. We are creatures of temporality, always having the potential at any moment to experience past, present, and future as a unity. This is what occurs between the therapist and patient while being in the moment. Emotional growth is predicated on this unity. The affective moment of emotional growth provides us with a glimpse into our true nature as temporality. It is vital to realize that "temporality" is not a fixed state or condition of the human being. "Temporality" opens up the possibility of an awareness of what it means to "be" human in the process of becoming. Lear concurs with this conclusion by noting:

> This would seem to leave open the possibility that the I
> is ever in the process of development. Indeed, Freud sug
> gests this when he lays down his memorable phrase for
> the task of psychoanalysis: Where id was, there ego shall
> be. Or, more accurately and more hauntingly: Where it
> was, there I shall become. This would seem to suggest
> that the project of becoming an I is the essential human
> task, and that psychoanalysis is an integral part of that
> project. (Lear, 2003, pp. 76–77)

Emotional growth ultimately puts old ghosts, having tyrannized the ego for years, to rest. In terms of the effort here, it means confronting the unconscious assassin for what it is and rendering it powerless. In the end, it appears to be a Herculean task. It is the means by which Paul Morel might have dared to separate from his mother and pursue a world of his own. It offers encouragement to others like him to engage in this kind of positive therapeutic involvement.

Reconciling profound loss is an essential dimension of the process of emerging from the narcissistic drama. The incentive for all of this effort is the prospect of living autonomously. It is true that Paul, even with the benefit of treatment, would have to carry a sense of emptiness pertaining to his distorted maternal relationship throughout his life. But, at the same time, he would conceivably have had a chance to advance a life of his own—that is pursuing the work and love that would come to define it. It would render all of his suffering and struggle to rejuvenate worthwhile.

* * *

Ludwig Binswanger

Having raised the issue, it is important in the end to discuss the relevance and significance of Heidegger's philosophy for psychotherapy. Though it may seem surprising in this context, Heidegger never intended for his thought to provide a foundation for any kind of psychology. He would regard this application as a distracting byproduct or, at best, a diversion from his original quest. His primary aim in writing *Being and Time* was to reveal the meaning of being. His focus on the being of human being represented a technical maneuver that was never meant to contribute to an understanding of what it means to be a person. Heidegger was a German philosopher who wrote in the early twentieth century. His philosophy was meant to critically respond to philosophical tradition and uplift knowledge about truth itself.

The area of Heidegger's concern is ontology or the science of being. His claim was that the meaning of being, a concern originally pursued in the quest for truth by Pre-Socratic philosophers, has been forgotten for millennia. He viewed himself as resurrecting the Pre-Socratic search for truth. His basic observation is that the meaning of being in the modern era had become empty and vacuous. Language is infused with the concept of being and, yet, no one can truly say what the concept of being means. Language and thought for Heidegger had become alienated from their ontological roots. He undertook the project of returning to the meaning of being in order to reveal "truth itself".

Heidegger does not consider truth to be the colloquial modern search for absolute certainty or rooted in explanations of causality. Rather, he maintains the Pre-Socratic view that truth has been covered over by time and misguided thinking. Therefore, the philosopher's task is to discover truth by uncovering it. For Heidegger, then, truth is defined by the Greek word, "aletheia", meaning unhiddenness. He allied himself with the Pre-Socratic philosopher, Heraclitus, who is credited with having said, "Nature loves to hide" (Heraclitus, fragment 123, in Hyland (1973) p. 170). In other words, truth is concealed and needs to be revealed through ontological investigation. Heidegger, consequently, assumed the role of a modern shepherd watching over the process of revealing the meaning of being.

In an effort to reveal the meaning of being and to initiate his project, Heidegger set out to gain the most effective access to "Being Itself". He concluded that the best means of access from an ontological perspective would be to investigate the being for which Being is an issue. He chose to focus on human being as the only being known to be concerned with this enquiry. He postulated that, through analyzing the being of human being, one might intelligibly reach the horizon of "Being Itself". Another formulation is that by disclosing the being of human being, one might gain a glimpse into "Being Itself". This reasoning guided the process of pursuing a phenomenology of human being. In *Being and Time*, he developed a brilliant characterization of human being that would later be modified by others as the basis for a psychotherapeutic approach. He referred to his ontological analysis of human being as "Daseinanalytik".

The concept of being is inextricably bound to the concept of existence. It is axiomatic that a being exists. Therefore, ontological enquiry is necessarily existential. Existential considerations converge on living, dying, and one's possibilities for being in the face of both.

The concept of time lends itself to an understanding of Heidegger's ontological point of view. Clock-time is seen as derivative and lived time as primordial. "Primordial time is contrasted with 'world time' as the public temporalizing of temporality. Public dating is marked by measurement of time and created the necessary devices for its task in calendars and especially clocks. Clock-time, created by Temporality for its own ontic purposes, can only be seen as derivative. Moreover, with regard to measurement, clock-time represents the encroachment of spatiality over primordial temporality" (Feinberg, 1977, p. 75). Lived time represents the essence of human being while clock-time is an artifact, a creation of convenience. "Preoccupied with schedules and dead-lines, irresolute Dasein 'has no time' in its rushing existence. On the other hand, resolute Dasein, which is aware of primordial time, 'has time' which fills its existence" (Feinberg, 1977, p. 75). For Heidegger, lived time is ontological while clock-time is not. Heidegger referred to phenomena that are not ontological as ontic.

What predisposes Heidegger's philosophy towards psychotherapy is the emphasis on states-of-mind or moods. His thought is unique in the history of philosophy for its central focus on moods. He maintained that human being or Dasein reveals its true nature through moods. His view is that the particular mood that captures the essential being of Dasein is *Angst*. Although the word "*Angst*" is commonly translated as anxiety, it is far more complex for Heidegger than what is colloquially known as anxiety. It is one of the core concepts in *Being and Time* that defies simple definition. From an ontological perspective, "*Angst*" is more of an individualizing process that centers on Dasein's authentic encounter with mortality.

Heidegger affirmed that it is only through "*Angst*" that the meaning of being of human being is uncovered. Therefore, "*Angst*" is seen as a potential conduit to glimpsing the meaning of "Being Itself".

Ludwig Binswanger, a Swiss psychiatrist of the early and middle twentieth century, had the vision to transform Heidegger's "Daseinanalytik" into the theoretical foundation of a novel approach to psychotherapy. He called it "Daseinanalyse" or existential analysis. Although inspired by *Being and Time*, Binswanger conceived of existential analysis as distinct from Heidegger's ontological project. Its aim was to develop a new understanding of human experience and the workings of the mind. Binswanger's position is expressed in the following passage: "However, existential analysis itself is neither an ontology nor a philosophy and, therefore, must refuse to be termed a *philosophical anthropology*; as the reader will soon realize, only the designation of *phenomenological anthropology* meets the fact of the situation" (Binswanger, 1958c, in R. May (Ed.), 1958, p. 194). By the term, "anthropology", he is referring to the study of mankind in a broad sense. In this way, his theory sought to offer an approach to psychiatric disorders that provided an alternative to psychoanalysis. The existential analytic critique of psychoanalysis is fundamentally based on the observation that the tenets of psychoanalysis are mechanistic in reifying human being and upholding the age-old duality of mind and body. In other words, psychoanalysis basically regards human being as an object with agencies and subparts. This stance is in sharp contrast to existential analysis in which the being of human being is preserved and not reified.

Despite the sharp theoretical divide in presuppositions between existential analysis and psychoanalysis, Binswanger and Freud maintained a longstanding friendship (Binswanger, 1957). They shared an enduring sense of mutual respect. Freud was twenty-five years older than Binswanger. Binswanger always acknowledged Freud's greatness as a scientific pioneer uncovering the workings of the mind. It is interesting to note that while many early disciples, such as Carl Jung, broke from Freud, Binswanger remained forever personally loyal to him as a colleague and friend.

It is accurate to say that Binswanger did not reject psychoanalysis as a methodology per se. Rather, he held that psychoanalysis was beneficial in addressing dimensions of human being but not sufficient in characterizing human being as a totality. Binswanger viewed human being as consisting of three dimensions: the "Mitwelt" (Dasein in its relation to others), the "Eigenwelt" (Dasein in relation to itself, including spirituality) and the "Umwelt" (Dasein's biological condition and the surrounding environment). He maintained that psychoanalysis can be appropriately applied to the Umwelt but does not take into account the Mitwelt or Eigenwelt. As a result, Binswanger employed psychoanalytic interpretation and technique as indicated within the larger context of existential analysis.

While acknowledging his debt to *Being and Time*, it was astute of Binswanger to realize that it was vital to diverge from Heidegger's thought in order to found existential analysis. He referred to this divergence as a "creative misinterpretation" of Heideggerian canon. Whereas Heidegger held Dasein's essence to be individualized and non-relational, Binswanger's position was that Dasein is fundamentally relational. There is no possibility of founding a psychotherapeutic approach on a rigid and strict reading of *Being and Time* for two basic reasons. First, others are seen as obstructing the individualization of Dasein in *Angst*. The quintessence of this view is witnessed at the end of Sartre's play, *No Exit*, which concludes with the statement "Hell is—other people!" (Sartre, 1948, p. 47). Second, what constitutes authentic speech for Heidegger is silence. While silence has an important place in psychotherapy, it is necessary for some kind of authentic exchange to occur in speech. Binswanger adapted the approach of *Being and Time* to a conception of human being as essentially relational. May makes the following observation in support of Binswanger's relational perspective: "Though we can not go into this complex topic, we can at least say that knowing another human being, like loving him, involves a kind of union, a dialectical participation with the other. This Binswanger calls the 'dual mode'. One must have at least a readiness to love the other person, broadly speaking, if one is to be able to understand him" (May, 1958, p. 38).

While Heidegger provided intellectual scaffolding for Binswanger, his spiritual indebtedness must be attributed to Martin Buber. Buber, of course, is the Jewish theologian renowned for his great poetically religious work, *I and Thou*. Binswanger's "dual mode" is akin to Buber's notion of reciprocity. He shared Buber's view of human being as fundamentally relational and the conviction that "relation is reciprocity" (Buber, 1923, p. 58). For both Binswanger and Buber, a person is never an object or a thing characterized solely by measurement, mechanics, energy regulation, and impulses. The ontological and spiritual essence of human being as relational must be apprehended and respected for the sake of a profound sense of reality. The alternative is reification and emptiness. It is clear that Binswanger's humanity is allied with Buber's values.

Binswanger's humanitarian nature prevented him from falling into the moral abyss that claimed Heidegger. It is both shocking and disconcerting that *Being and Time* lacked the moral safeguards necessary to keep Heidegger from becoming affiliated with the Nazi Party. He gave speeches supporting Hitler and obtained coveted academic appointments as a result. Although Heidegger belatedly renounced his alignment with the Nazis, his reputation and the stature of his philosophy had been forever tarnished. Binswanger's creative misinterpretation of central tenets of *Being and Time* added spiritual and moral dimension to Heidegger's thought. Binswanger's efforts, drawing on the influence of Buber, ultimately render Heidegger's project humane and compatible with the authentic reciprocity of love, and it is this sense of love that underlies his understanding of existential analysis. It is unfortunate that Heidegger, in the end, did endorse only those psychological adaptations of his philosophy that strictly and faithfully adhered to his ideas. By dismissing Binswanger, Heidegger sacrificed an opportunity at redemption and reparation.

It is somewhat ironic that Binswanger and his priorities have been forgotten in much the same way Heidegger brought attention to Being having been forgotten. Modern psychiatry and psychology generally operate within a constricted scientific field of understanding human being. The primary locus of clinical concern is to be found in measurement, neurophysiology, and brain chemistry to the exclusion of regarding human being as a whole. Instead of striving to comprehend the lived experience of those with mental disorders, psychiatric assessments nowadays center on medication evaluation to manage symptoms and descriptors from a statistical manual. For Binswanger, this picture can only reveal alienation from awareness of what it means to be human. Gabriel Marcel, the twentieth-century Christian existential philosopher, perfectly portrayed the value on reciprocity held by Binswanger in the following passage about his concept of availability:

> It is an undeniable fact, though it is hard to describe in intelligible terms, that there are some people who reveal themselves as 'present'—that is to say, at our disposal—when we are in pain or need to confide in someone, while there are other people who do not give us this feeling, however great their goodwill. It should be noted at once that the distinction between presence and absence is not at all the same as that between attention and distraction. The most attentive and the most conscientious listener may give me the impression of not being present; he gives

me nothing, he cannot make room for me in himself, whatever the material favors he is prepared to grant me. The truth is that there is a way of listening which is a way of giving, and another way of listening which is a way of refusing, of refusing *oneself*; the material gift, the visual action, do not necessarily witness to presence. We must not speak of proof in this connection; the word would be out of place, Presence is something which reveals itself immediately and unmistakably in a look, a smile, an intonation or a hand-shake. (Marcel, 1956, pp. 39–40)

REFERENCES

Binswanger, L. (1957). *Sigmund Freud: Reminiscences of a Friendship.* (Trans). N. Guterman. New York: Grune & Stratton.

Binswanger, L. (1958c). The existential analysis school of thought. (Trans.) by E. Angel. In: R. May, E. Angel & H. Ellenberger (Eds.), *Existence: A New Dimension in Psychiatry and Psychology* (pp. 191–213). New York: Basic Books.

Blanck, G. & Blanck, R. (1974). *Ego Psychology: Theory and Practice.* New York: Columbia University Press.

Blos, P. (1967). The second individuation process of adolescence. *The Psychoanalytic Study of the Child, 22*: 162–186.

Buber, M. (1923). *I and Thou.* (Trans.) by W. Kaufmann. New York: Charles Scribner's Sons. 1970.

Chayevsky, P. (1976). *Network.* Directed by S. Lumet. Produced by Metro-Goldwyn-Mayer.

Considine, S. (1994). *Mad As Hell: The Life and Work of Paddy Chayevsky.* New York: Random House.

Descartes, R. (1641). *Meditation on First Philosophy* in *Descartes: Philosophical Writings* (Trans. by N. K. Smith). New York: The Modern Library. 1958.

Erikson, E. H. (1959). *Identity and The Life Cycle.* New York: W. W. Norton.

Feinberg, R. I. (1977). Heidegger's thought and the existential analytic movement in psychiatry: A study of their relation with a critique of humanism. Unpublished honors thesis in Philosophy. Hartford, CT: Trinity College.

Feinberg, R. I. (1997). Adaptation to mortality at the stage of integrity vs. despair: A case for the synthesis of psychoanalytic and existential perspectives on the nature of maturity in the later years. *Journal of Aging and Identity*, 2: 37–58.

Freud, S. (1900). *The Interpretation of Dreams. S. E.*, 4: 1–623. London: Hogarth Press. 1953.

Freud, S. (1905). On psychotherapy. *S. E.*, 7: 257–268. London: Hogarth Press. 1953.

Freud, S. (1914a). *On Narcissism: An Introduction. S. E.*, 14: 73–102. London: Hogarth Press. 1953.

Freud, S. (1914e). The Unconscious. *S. E., 14*: 166–204. London: Hogarth Press. 1953.

Freud, S. (1916). On Transference. *S. E., 14*: 305–307. London: Hogarth Press. 1953.

Greenberg, J. & Mitchell, S. (Eds.) (1983). *Object Relations in Psychoanalytic Theory*. Cambridge, MA: Harvard University Press.

Heidegger, M. (1927). *Being and Time*. (Trans.) by J. Macquarrie & E. Robinson. New York: Harper & Row. 1962.

Heraclitus. Fragment 123. In: Hyland, D. A. (1973). *The Origins of Philosophy*. (Trans.) by D. A. Hyland. New York: G. P. Putnam's Sons.

Hitchcock, A. (1960). *Psycho*. Shamely Productions.

Husserl, E. (1911). *Phenomenology and the Crisis of Philosophy*. (Trans.) by Q. Lauer. New York: Harper & Row. 1965.

Kafka, F. (1914). *The Metamorphosis*. (Trans.) by S. Corngold. New York: Bantam Books. 1972.

Kafka, F. (1917). *The Trial*. (Trans.) by W. Muir & E. Muir. New York: Alfred A. Knopf. 1937.

Kierkegaard, S. (1843). *Fear and Trembling and The Sickness Unto Death*. (Trans.) by W. Lowrie. Princeton University Press. 1941.

Lawrence, D. H. (1913). *Sons and Lovers*. New York: William Heinemann. 1979.

Lawrence, D. H. (1926). *The Rocking-horse Winner*, In: *The Complete Short Stories of D. H. Lawrence*, Vol. III. Copyright 1933 by The Estate of D. H. Lawrence. Reprinted with permission by The Viking Press.

Lear, J. (2003). *Therapeutic Action: An Earnest Plea for Irony*. London: Karnac.

Little, W., Fowler, H. W., Coulson, J. & Onions, C. T. (Eds.) (1972). *The Shorter Oxford English Dictionary on Historical Principles*, 3rd edition. Oxford: Oxford University Press.

Loewald, H. (1960). On the therapeutic action of psycho-analysis. *International Journal of Psycho-Analysis 41*: 16–33.

Mahler, M. S., Pine, F. & Bergmann, A. (1975). *The Psychological Birth of the Human Infant*. New York: Basic Books.

Marcel, G. (1956). On the ontological mystery. In: *The Philosophy of Existentialism*. (pp. 9–46). (Trans.) by M. Harari. Secaucus, N.J.: The Citadel Press.

May, R. (1958). Contributions to existential psychotherapy in *existence*. In: R. May, E. Angel & H. Ellenburger (Eds.), *A New Dimension in Psychiatry and Psychology* (pp. 37–91). New York: Basic Books. 1958.

Miller, A. (1981). *The Drama of the Gifted Child*. New York: Basic Books.

Ovid (1 A.C.E.). *Metamorphoses*, Book III. (Trans.) by M. M. Innes. London: Penguin Books. 1955.

Plato. *The Apology*. (Trans.) by W. H. D. Rouse. In: *Great Dialogues of Plato*. New York: The New American Library. 1956.

Rosen, S. (1968). *Plato's Symposium*. New Haven: Yale University Press.

Ruderman, J. (1984). *D. H. Lawrence and the Devouring Mother: The Search for a Patriarchal Ideal of Leadership*. Durham, N.C.: Duke University Press.

The New York Times (2012). Adrienne Rich, Feminist Poet, Dies at 82, 28 March 2012. published by The New York Times Co.

Winnicott, D. W. (1947). Hate in the countertransference. In: *Through Paediatrics to Psycho-Analysis*. (pp. 194–203). New York: Basic Books. 1975.

Winnicott, D. W. (1960). Ego distortion in terms of the true and false self. In: *The Maturational Processes and the Facilitating Environment*. (pp. 140–152). London: Hogarth Press. 1979.

INDEX